TOP **10**
DUBLIN

POLLY PHILLIMORE
&
ANDREW SANGER

DK

EYEWITNESS TRAVEL

Left **Four Courts** Right **Horse carriages, Killarney**

LONDON, NEW YORK,
MELBOURNE, MUNICH AND DELHI
www.dk.com

Produced by Sargasso Media Ltd, London

Printed and bound in China

First American Edition, 2003
14 15 16 17 10 9 8 7 6 5 4 3 2 1

Published in the United States by
Dorling Kindersley Publishing, Inc.,
345 Hudson Street, New York 10014

A Penguin Random House Company

Copyright 2003, 2015 © Dorling Kindersley
Limited, London

**Reprinted with revisions
2005, 2007, 2009, 2011, 2013, 2015**

Published in the UK by
Dorling Kindersley Limited.

A catalog record for this book is available
from the Library of Congress.

ISSN 1479-344X
ISBN 978-1-46540-987-4

Within each Top 10 list in this book, no hierarchy
of quality or popularity is implied. All 10 are, in
the editor's opinion, of roughly equal merit.

MIX
Paper from
responsible sources
FSC™ C018179
www.fsc.org

Contents

Dublin's Top 10

Trinity College   8

National Museum
of Ireland   10

National Gallery of Ireland   12

Dublin Castle   14

Temple Bar   18

Christ Church Cathedral   20

St Patrick's Cathedral   22

Guinness Storehouse   24

Kilmainham Gaol
and Hospital   26

Phoenix Park   28

Moments in History   30

Historic Buildings   32

Dublin Writers   34

Children's Attractions   36

Cover: Front – **AWL Images** Travel Pix collection main; **Dorling Kindersley** Magnus Rew bl. Spine – **Dorling
Kindersley:** Alan Williams b. Back – **Dorling Kindersley** Tim Draly tr; Alan Williams tl, tc.

Left **Glendalough** Right **Rock of Dunamase**

Sporting Events 37

Legends and Myths 38

Performing Arts Venues 40

Pubs 42

Nightspots 44

Shopping Areas 46

Restaurants 48

Around Town

South of the Liffey 52

North of the Liffey 60

Greater Dublin 68

Around Ireland

Wicklow Mountains 80

Around Waterford 82

Ring of Kerry and Dingle
Peninsula 86

Around Cork 90

Tipperary, Limerick
and Clare 94

Clonmacnoise and the
Midlands 98

Around Galway 100

Connemara and Mayo 104

Yeats Country
and the Northwest 108

Northern Ireland 114

Streetsmart

Practical Information 120

Places to Stay 128

General Index 136

Left **Powerscourt Gardens** Right **Grafton Street**

Key to abbreviations
Adm *admission charge* **Free** *no admission charge* **Dis. access** *disabled access*

3

DUBLIN'S TOP10

Dublin Highlights
6–7

Trinity College
8–9

National Museum
of Ireland
10–11

National Gallery of
Ireland
12–13

Dublin Castle
14–17

Temple Bar
18–19

Christ Church
Cathedral
20–21

St Patrick's
Cathedral
22–23

Guinness
Storehouse
24–25

Kilmainham Gaol
and Hospital
26–27

Phoenix Park
28–29

Top Ten of Everything
30–49

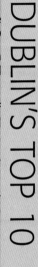

DUBLIN'S TOP 10

📕10 Dublin's Highlights

One of the most popular capitals in Europe, Dublin is a city steeped in history. Huddled together within a small vicinity you'll find Viking remains, medieval cathedrals and churches, Georgian squares and excellent museums. But it's not just about buildings – music, theatre, literature and pubs play just as strong a part in Dublin's atmosphere. These ten sights are the must-sees for any visitor who wants to truly capture the variety and vibrancy of the city.

Trinity College 📕
The elder statesman of Ireland's universities, Trinity is also one of the oldest in Europe. Its buildings and grounds are a landmark in the heart of the city *(see pp8–9).*

National Museum of Ireland 📕
Three collections in three locations make up this outstanding museum, ranging from dinosaurs to military history *(see pp10–11).*

Greater Dublin

National Gallery of Ireland 📕
Wonderful Italian, French, Dutch and Spanish works are exhibited here, alongside a great collection of Irish art *(see pp12–13).*

Dublin Castle 📕
A surprisingly peaceful area, the castle was built into the medieval walls of the city and originally protected by the River Liffey to the north and in the south and east by the now underground River Poddle *(see pp14–17).*

Christel Church Cathedral 6

Striking Norman, Gothic, Romanesque and Victorian features jostle for attention in this former Viking church *(see pp20–21)*.

5 Temple Bar

This ancient part of the city has been revamped into one of its busiest areas, day and night. There is no shortage of places to eat and drink *(see pp18–19)*.

7 St Patrick's Cathedral

Known colloquially as the "People's Cathedral", this is one of the earliest Christian sites in the city and is the Protestant community's main place of worship in the capital *(see pp22–3)*.

8 Guinness Storehouse

A pint of Guinness could be the country's national symbol. This fascinating exhibition at the Guinness Brewery ends with a welcome free pint of the famous black stuff in the sampling bar *(see pp24–5)*.

9 Kilmainham Gaol and Hospital

After a sobering tour of the one-time prison, lighten the mood at the former hospital, which now houses the Irish Museum of Modern Art *(see pp26–7)*.

10 Phoenix Park

The great pride and play area of Dubliners, this is one of the largest city parks in Europe. Historic monuments and Dublin Zoo are only a few of its delights *(see pp28–9)*.

Trinity College

Trinity College is Dublin's most famous educational institution and, since its foundation in the 16th century, has produced many impressive alumni, among them Jonathan Swift, William Congreve, Oliver Goldsmith, Oscar Wilde, Bram Stoker and Samuel Beckett. Situated on College Green, this was once part of the Priory of All Hallows grounds, but is unfortunately now a busy road junction. It is Trinity itself that provides the haven in this area. Entering through the West Front, under a wooden-tiled archway, is like walking into a bucolic time-warp: cobbled quadrangle, smooth green lawns and an array of fine 18th- and 19th-century buildings. A number of the buildings are open to the public, the most outstanding being the Old Library, home to one of the country's greatest treasures, the Book of Kells.

Façade

🔵 In South Frederick Street there's an excellent Italian delicatessen, Dunne & Crescenzi, serving delicious snacks, wine and coffee.

🟢 The exhibition "The Book of Kells: Turning Darkness into Light" explains the history and background to illuminated manuscripts. It includes full-scale reproductions of the *Book of Kells*.

- College Green
- Map F4
- 01-896 2308
- www.tcd.ie
- Library open Jun–Sep: 9:30am–5pm Mon–Sat, 9:30am–4:30pm Sun; Oct–May: 9:30am–5pm Mon–Sat, noon–4:30pm Sun
- Adm €9
- Dis. access

Top 10 Features

1. Front Arch
2. Campanile
3. Old Library
4. Book of Kells
5. Library Square
6. Chapel
7. Dining Hall
8. Museum Building
9. Berkeley Library Building
10. Douglas Hyde Gallery

Front Arch

College Green, facing the Front Arch entrance to Trinity, was originally called Hoggen Green. The statues of Edmund Burke and Oliver Goldsmith which flank the entrance are the work of sculptor John Foley.

Campanile

This 30-m (100-ft) bell-tower *(right)* is the centrepiece of Trinity's main quad, enclosed by fine 18th- and 19th-century buildings. Built by Sir Charles Lanyon, the architect of Queen's University in Belfast, in 1853, it marks the site of All Hallows monastery.

Old Library

Entry to the Old Library *(above)*, built between 1712 and 1732, is from Fellows' Square. The finest feature is the magnificent 64-m (200-ft) Long Room, with two tiers of antiquated oak bookcases holding more than 200,000 books. The barrel-vaulted ceiling was added in 1860. The collection grows yearly as Trinity is entitled to copies of all titles published in Ireland and the UK.

For more historic buildings in Dublin See pp32–3

Book Of Kells

This beautifully decorated illuminated manuscript is one of the city's most treasured possessions. It is thought to date from around AD 800 and is believed to be the work of monks from the island of Iona in Scotland. They moved to Kells in County Meath to escape Viking raids and the book was eventually given to Trinity by the Bishop of Meath in 1654.

Plan of Trinity College

Dining Hall

Just beside the chapel, this grand dining hall, where Trinity's many students eat, was originally built by Richard Cassels in 1742, but it has been considerably altered over the past 250 years. It has been totally restored after a fire in 1984 and the walls are hung with huge portraits of college dignitaries.

Museum Building

This fine Venetian-style building *(above)* was designed by Sir Thomas Deane and Benjamin Woodward and completed in 1857. Inside, a pair of giant Irish deer skeletons stand guard in the magnificent hall. The detailed decoration of smaller animals, birds and flowers was carved by the O'Shea brothers.

Library Square

On the east side of this photogenic square is a red-brick building known as the Rubrics. It was built around 1700 and is the oldest part of the college.

Chapel

The chapel, completed in 1798, is the only one in Ireland shared by all denominations. The fine stained-glass window *(right)* above the altar dates from 1867.

Berkeley Library Building

In front of Paul Koralek's 1967 creation is the sculpture *Sphere within a Sphere* (1982) by Arnaldo Pomodoro *(below)*.

Douglas Hyde Gallery

One of Ireland's leading contemporary art galleries, the Douglas Hyde has exhibitions by both emerging and well-established artists from Ireland and abroad.

The History of Trinity College

Founded in 1592 by Queen Elizabeth I on the site of All Hallows Augustinian Monastery, and modelled on the universities of Oxford and Cambridge, Trinity's objective was to provide young Protestants with an alternative to going to universities in Europe where they might fall under the influence of Catholicism. The Anglican bias lasted into the 1970s even though religious restrictions were abolished in 1793.

ᴛᴏᴘ10 National Museum of Ireland

There are three different parts to this huge and outstanding museum. The Kildare Street branch offers archaeology and history, as far back as prehistoric Ireland's early culture. The Merrion Street branch comprises the Museum of Natural History, colloquially known as "The Dead Zoo". The third branch of the museum, in Benburb Street, at the west end of the city, is the Decorative Arts and History, Collins Barracks; exhibits include The Way We Wore, a display of clothing and jewellery worn in Ireland from the 1760s to the 1960s. This branch of the museum is a very different experience, with the most up-to-date display techniques and interesting and varied collections portraying the country's decorative arts and social, military, economic and political history.

Museum of Natural History façade

🍴 The café at Collins Barracks is an excellent place to find refreshments. It is located in East Block, Clarke Square.

• Archaeology Museum: Kildare Street, Dublin 2; Natural History Museum: Merrion Street, Dublin 2; Decorative Arts and History, Collins Barracks: Benburb Street, Dublin 7
• Map F5
• 01-677 7444
• www.museum.ie
• Open 10am–5pm Tue–Sat, 2–5pm Sun
• Free
• Dis. access ground floor only (Natural History Museum and Archaeology Museum); full access (Collins Barracks)

Top 10 Exhibits

1. Façade
2. Or – Ireland's Gold
3. Treasury
4. Viking Collection
5. The Easter Rising
6. Prehistoric Ireland
7. Soldiers & Chiefs
8. Fonthill Vase
9. Irish Silver
10. What's In Store

Façade
The exterior of the museum in Kildare Street is an example of Victorian Palladian style, enhanced by renovation. The domed rotunda rises to a height of 20 m and is modelled on the Pantheon in Rome.

Or – Ireland's Gold
This outstanding collection of ancient gold *(below)* was found in various counties as far apart as County Clare and County Derry. The pieces show the level of skill and invention of Bronze Age artisans. (Archaeology Museum, Kildare Street)

Treasury
Part of a hoard found in County Limerick in 1808, the Ardagh Chalice is probably the museum's most famous object. The mid-8th-century chalice is a beautiful example of the Irish Early Christian metalworker's craft. Another beauty from this collection is the Tara Brooch. (Archaeology Museum, Kildare Street)

Viking Collection
Ireland's Viking Age extended from AD 800–1150 and part of this exhibition *(above)* concentrates on the warlike aspect of this period. The skeleton of a warrior was excavated from burial grounds around Kilmainham *(see pp26–7)*. (Archaeology Museum, Kildare Street)

The Easter Rising: Understanding 1916
This exhibition covers the period of unrest between 1913 and 1923, from the Dublin Lockout, through the Easter Rising to the end of the Civil War. It is an examination of the social and economic background to the Rising. (Decorative Arts & History, Collins Barracks)

Prehistoric Ireland
The Lurgan Longboat, dating from around 2500 BC, is made out of hollowed-out oak trunks and 15 m (50 ft) long. Other pieces include the cast bronze horns, probably played like the Australian didgeridoo, and a range of prehistoric pots *(below)*. (Archaeology Museum, Kildare Street)

Soldiers & Chiefs
This exhibition displays over 1,000 military artifacts. Firearms, swords, letters and uniforms from the 16th to the 21st century retell the stories of Irish men and women at war. Highlights include Padraig Pearse's pistol from 1916 and a UN armoured vehicle *(left)*. (Decorative Arts & History, Collins Barracks)

Fonthill Vase
This vase *(below)* is the only surviving example of porcelain to have left China in the 14th century and whose history can be traced from that moment on. (Decorative Arts & History, Collins Barracks)

Irish Silver
The silver collection ranges from the 17th to 20th centuries and shows a huge variety of styles. The arrival of French Huguenot silversmiths in Dublin had a strong influence on local design. (Decorative Arts & History, Collins Barracks)

What's In Store
This wonderful exhibit is one of the highlights of the converted Decorative Arts and History, Collins Barracks branch of the museum. A visible storage display, it makes more than 16,000 objects from the decorative arts collection accessible to the public in one space.

Museum Guide

If you want to visit all three parts of the National Museum on the same day, start with the Natural History Museum in Merrion Square. The Archaeology Museum is only a few minutes' walk from here but there is a tourist Hop-on-Hop-off bus that will take you from one to the other. If you're walking, turn right at the lights on Baggot Street. Walk along the north side of St Stephen's Green, turn right into Kildare Street to the Archaeology Museum. From here to the third wing, Collins Barracks, take the tourist bus to the north of the river.

National Gallery of Ireland

The National Gallery's outstanding collection of Western European art ranges from the Middle Ages to the mid-20th century and includes, as one might expect in the nation's capital, the most important gathering of Irish art in the world. The gallery was designed by architect Francis Fowke (1823–65) and opened in January 1864. The Milltown Wing was added in 1903, the Beit Wing in 1968 and the Millennium Wing in 2002, the last bringing a huge improvement in exhibition space and public facilities. The gallery has had some important donors during its history, including Countess Milltown, George Bernard Shaw (see p34), Sir Hugh Lane, Chester Beatty (see p17) and Sir Alfred and Lady Beit. The Gallery is currently preparing for a major refurbishment of the Dargan and Milltown Wings and the upper Millennium Wing is closed until 2016.

Entrance to The Millennium Wing

🍴 The Café is a beautiful space to enjoy hot dishes, soups and salads or just coffee and a cake. There is a large open-plan space at the Clare Street entrance which is the self-service restaurant.

- Clare St & Merrion Square, Dublin 2
- Map G5
- 01-661 5133
- www.nationalgallery.ie
- Open 9:30am–5:30pm Mon–Wed, Fri–Sat, 9:30am–8:30pm Thu, noon–5:30pm Sun
- Dis. access
- Free

Top 10 Collections

1. Yeats Archive
2. Irish Art
3. British School
4. Italian Painting
5. French Painting
6. Spanish Painting
7. German, Dutch and Flemish Painting
8. Baroque Rooms
9. Prints and Drawings
10. The Millennium Wing

Yeats Archive

This exceptional collection includes portraits of the Yeats family as well as an impressive group of Jack B Yeats's paintings, from early favourites such as *The Liffey Swim* (1923) *(below)* to later expressionistic work such as *Grief* (1951).

Irish Art

Six rooms do justice to this extensive collection devoted to 18th- and 19th-century Irish art. Works by James Barry *(above)* are representative of the 18th century, while Nathaniel Hone the Younger begins the transition to the Impressionists, represented by Roderic O'Conor and Walter Frederick Osborne.

British School
3 Paintings in this school span from the Tudor period to the early 20th century with a particularly good 18th-century section. Hogarth, Reynolds, Romney, Gainsborough and Raeburn are particularly well represented.

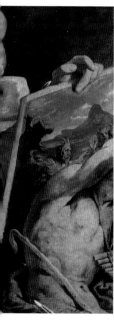

Italian Painting
4 The lovely Italian collection ranges from the Renaissance to the 18th century. Caravaggio's *The Taking of Christ* (1602) is the most outstanding piece in the 17th-century works of art.

French Painting
5 Monet's *Argenteuil Basin with a Single Sailboat* (1874) *(right)* is one of the highlights of the French collection, most of which dates from the 17th to the 19th centuries.

Spanish Painting
6 Goya and Velázquez are among many great artists in this collection, which concentrates on the 17th century and includes *Kitchen Maid with the Supper at Emmaus (above)*. The modern era is represented by Picasso's *Still Life with a Mandolin* (1924).

German, Dutch and Flemish Painting
7 An interesting painting in the Flemish collection is a collaborative work, *Christ in the House of Martha and Mary* (1628), with figures by Peter Paul Rubens set in a Jan Brueghel II landscape *(above)*.

Baroque Rooms
8 The Baroque collection is divided in two parts. Room 44 has the Baroque Italian, Spanish, French and Flemish paintings from the 17th and 18th centuries. Room 26 is a gallery devoted to the Baroque age in Italy.

Prints and Drawings
9 This extensive collection includes simple pencil sketches, preparatory studies for paintings, landscape watercolours and architectural drawings. A highlight is the collection of 18th-century Dublin streetscapes by James Mahoney.

The Millennium Wing
10 The main galleries added at the first level of this wing concentrate on modern Irish art, showing the rise of Modernism (rooms 1–5). The upper Millennium room will be closed until 2016. See the gallery's website for more information.

Gallery Guide

The National Gallery has four wings on four levels: the Dargan Wing, the Milltown Wing, the Beit Wing and the Millennium Wing. Each wing has colour-coded signs to help visitors find their way around. There are facilities for wheelchair users and a special floorplan in "Green, marked Access", which shows the location of all the lifts and ramps. Many of the gallery's exhibits can be viewed by appointment only. Parts of the gallery will be closed for refurbishment until 2016. Visit the gallery's website for more detailed information.

🔟 Dublin Castle

The appropriately imposing structure of Dublin Castle was a controversial symbol of British rule for 700 years, until it was formally handed over to Michael Collins and the Irish Free State in 1922 (see p31). Commissioned by King John in the 13th century, over the years the castle evolved from a medieval fortress into a vice-regal court and administrative centre. It has suffered numerous tribulations in its history, but the most concerted attack was in 1534, when it was besieged by "Silken Thomas" Fitzgerald (so called for his finely embroidered wardrobe), a rebellious courtier who had renounced his allegiance to the English Crown. Its current use is primarily ceremonial. Visitors can tour the ornate state apartments and wander freely around the courtyards and museums.

Façade

🍴 The Silk Road Café beside the Chester Beatty Library has a great setting and serves dishes inspired by the countries featured in the library's collections.

ℹ️ The state apartments are closed to the public when a foreign dignitary is visiting or a national ceremonial is taking place, so check in advance.

- Dame Street, Dublin 2
- Map D4
- 01-645 8800
- www.dublincastle.ie
- Castle: Open 10am–4:45pm Mon–Sat, noon–4:45pm Sun; Chester Beatty Library (01-407 0750): open May–Sep: 10am–5pm Mon–Fri, 11am–5pm Sat, 1–5pm Sun; Oct–Apr: 10am–5pm Tue–Fri, 11am–5pm Sat, 1–5pm Sun
- Dis. access
- Free

Top 10 Features

1. Chester Beatty Library and Gallery
2. Figure of Justice
3. Bedford Tower
4. The Chapel Royal
5. Viking Undercroft
6. The Throne Room
7. Berminngham Tower Room
8. St Patrick's Hall
9. Gardens
10. The Revenue Museum

1 The Chester Beatty Library and Gallery

A stunning collection of artistic, religious and secular works from around the world dating from about 2700 BC to the present century *(see pp16–17)*.

2 Figure of Justice

Approaching the castle from Cork Hill, the Figure of Justice *(above)* guards the main entrance. It faces the Upper Yard, turning its back on the city – as Dubliners cynically commented, an apt symbol of British justice.

3 The Bedford Tower

The Norman gate of the original castle is the base for this attractive 18th-century clock tower *(below)*. In 1907, the Irish "Crown Jewels" – a diamond St Patrick Star and Badge – were stolen from here and never recovered.

The Chapel Royal
The exterior of this Neo-Gothic delight is decorated with more than 100 heads beautifully carved out of Tullamore limestone.

Viking Undercroft
Medieval excavations show the remains of the original castle, including part of a 9th-century Viking town and the moat on the river Poddle.

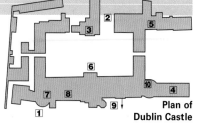

Plan of Dublin Castle

Bermingham Tower Room
This former medieval prison was converted into a state apartment.

Gardens
To the back of the chapel are the charming and peaceful Dubh Linn Gardens *(below)*, which are located on the site of the "Black Pool" harbour from which the city gets its name.

The Revenue Museum
Located in the crypt of the Chapel Royal, the exhibits here include a home-made still used to distil poitín, as well as interesting examples of counterfeit goods.

St Patrick's Hall
The hall, dedicated to Ireland's patron saint *(below)*, has ceiling paintings by Vincenzo Valdre (1742–1814) depicting incidents in British and Irish history, such as St Patrick lighting the Pascal Fire on the Hill of Slane.

Building Dublin Castle

In 1204, 30 years after the Anglo-Norman landing in Ireland, King John ordered a castle to be built in Dublin. The site found was the highest ground southeast of the existing town and protected on the east and south side by what was once the River Poddle. Much of this medieval castle was destroyed by fire in 1684 and Sir William Robinson completed the new apartments by 1688. Again, most of these were replaced in the 18th century.

The Throne Room
As its name suggests, this is the grandest state apartment in the castle. The throne *(above)* is flanked by four roundels and ovals depicting Minerva, Jupiter, Juno and Mars. They are attributed to Gaetano Gandolfi, an 18th-century Italian artist.

Left **Qur'an** Right **Japanese woodblock print**

Chester Beatty Library Guide

1 The Qur'an Collection
This gathering of more than 260 Qur'ans and Qur'an fragments is considered to be the most important of its kind outside the Middle East. Ibn al-Bawwab is reputed to be one of the greatest medieval Islamic calligraphers and displayed here is the exquisite Qur'an he copied in Baghdad in AD 1001.

2 Illuminated Manuscripts
Fine illuminated manuscripts can be found throughout the library, but the illustration of the Rose Garden of Sa'di, made in the 1420s for Baysunghur, a prince of the Timurid dynasty that ruled much of Iran in the 15th century, is one of the most beautiful.

3 Mughal-era Indian Collection
This collection includes some of the best paintings produced under the guidance of emperors Akbar, Shah Jahan and Jahangir.

4 Papyrus Texts
Papyrus is an aquatic plant from which ancient Egyptians made writing materials for their documents. One of the finest here is Paul's Letter to the Romans (c.AD 180–200). The hieroglyphic and demotic papyri relate to administrative and burial practices.

5 Japanese Inrō
These tiny, intricate boxes were used to store seals and medicines and are reproduced today by some perfumiers.

6 Chinese Collection
This eclectic display from the Qing dynasty includes snuff bottles, jade books, and a stunning range of silk dragon robes.

7 Japanese Picture Books
Some of the finest pieces in the Japanese collection are the painted handscrolls and albums of a type known as *Nara Ehon* (Nara picture books).

8 The Persian Poets
For connoisseurs of Persian poetry, Firdawsi, Nizami, Hafiz and Jami are just four of the authors of the 330 manuscripts.

9 Woodblocks
The *ukiyo-e* woodblock prints complement the outstanding set of more than 700 prints known as *surimono*. These prints, like modern-day greeting cards, were created to mark special events or occasions.

10 Bust of Chester Beatty
A bust of Chester Beatty by the sculptor Carolyn Mulholland is on display in the atrium.

Chinese dragon robe

Top 10 Artifacts

1. Paul's Letter to the Romans c.AD 180–200 (Western collection)
2. Illuminated initial H, c.AD 1153 *Walsingham Bible*, (Western collection)
3. Egyptian love poems, 1160 BC (Western collection)
4. *Scenes from a Noh Play*, 17th century (East Asian collection)
5. Qur'an, copied by Ibn al-Bawwab, AD 1001 (Islamic collection)
6. *The Tale of Oriole*, late 17th century (East Asian collection)
7. Luke 6: 30-41, Four Gospels and the Acts of the Apostles, AD 200–250
8. *The Madonna on a Grassy Bank*, Albrecht Dürer, AD 1503 (Western collection)
9. Jade snuff bottle, c.AD 1750–1800 (East Asian collection)
10. The Roleau Vase, early 18th century (East Asian collection) (Displays change frequently. Check website for details.)

Alfred Chester Beatty

Sir Alfred Chester Beatty

Alfred Chester Beatty was born in New York in 1875, and spent much of his childhood collecting stamps, minerals and Chinese snuff bottles. In adulthood, with a highly successful mining consultancy as his profession, he could afford to pursue his interests and eventually gathered together this outstanding collection of Islamic manuscripts, Chinese, Japanese and other Oriental Art. Beatty lived and worked in both New York and London before finally deciding to settle in Dublin in 1950. He built the first library for his precious collection on Shrewsbury Road, which was improved and added to over the years, before finally relocating to Dublin Castle in 2000. Beatty loved Ireland and contributed generously to its many galleries and cultural institutions. In 1957 he became the country's first honorary citizen, and decided that he would leave his library in trust for the benefit of the public. He died in 1968 and, in recognition of his great contribution to Irish life, he was accorded a state funeral – the only private citizen ever to have received such an honour.

Chinese Jade
This exquisite 18th-century jade book, inlaid with gold and entitled *The Perfection of the Wisdom of Sutra*, is a striking example of Beatty's eye for priceless Far Eastern art.

Temple Bar

A lively enclave of cafés, bars and theatres, the Temple Bar area covers the network of cobbled streets that stretch between Dame Street and the River Liffey, and from Fishamble Street to Fleet Street. Named after the 17th-century developer Sir William Temple, the area has gone full circle in its fortunes but is now firmly established as the city's most popular spot for tourists and locals alike. Known as Dublin's cultural quarter, there is something going on here throughout the year, but summer and autumn are definitely the high points. Summer brings a full programme of cultural events, including outdoor film screenings, street theatre and live music. The Dublin Theatre Festival, Culture Night and Fringe Festival bring the district to life throughout autumn.

City Hall

❷ Temple Bar is filled with cafés, pubs, restaurants and bars, most of them open from breakfast until after midnight.

❷ People come into Dublin especially for the Saturday Food Market, which starts at 10am in Meeting House Square and runs until late afternoon, so arrive early for the most choice.

• Map E4
• www.templebar.ie
• City Hall: Lord Edward St; Open 10am–5.15pm Mon–Sat; Adm €4 (for exhibition)
• Gallery of Photography: Meeting House Sq; Open 11am–6pm Tue–Sat, 1pm–6pm Sun; Free
• National Photographic Archive: Meeting House Sq; Visits by appointment only; Free
• Project Arts Centre: 39 Essex St East; Open Mon–Sat; Performances nightly
• Irish Film Institute: 6 Eustace St; Open daily

Top 10 Features

1. City Hall
2. Millennium Bridge
3. Merchant's Arch
4. Meeting House Square
5. The Ark
6. Cow's Lane
7. Gallery of Photography
8. National Photographic Archive
9. Project Arts Centre
10. Irish Film Institute

City Hall
Built by Thomas Cooley between 1769 and 1779, the building was originally designed to be the Royal Exchange, but political events led to a change of usage in the mid-19th century. Built of Portland stone, with a magnificent Rotunda entrance hall, it is an outstanding example of Neo-Classical style *(see p54).*

Millennium Bridge
One of three pedestrian bridges to cross the Liffey, its simple lines perfectly complement its more famous and more ornate companion, the Ha'penny Bridge *(see p56).* Designed by architects Howley Harrington, the bridge is intended to increase links between shopping areas north and south of the Liffey.

Merchant's Arch
A formal entry point to the area, the arch *(below)* dates from the days when ships sailed right up the Liffey to dock and trade here with the local merchants.

Plan of Temple Bar

4 Meeting House Square

Named after a Quaker Meeting Hall, this is the centre of Temple Bar. It is the venue for concerts, outdoor film screenings, and the Saturday food market *(above)*. Café tables, spilling out onto the street from minute interiors, all add to the atmosphere.

6 Cow's Lane

This smart pedestrian street *(right)* has designer boutiques and chic coffee bars. Fashion, jewellery and gift stalls line the centre path at the Designer Mart every Saturday from spring to late autumn.

9 Project Arts Centre

This modern art centre, begun in 1966 as a three-week festival, has gained an international reputation for avant-garde theatre, dance, music, film and art *(see p41)*.

10 Irish Film Institute

Housing the offices of independent film organizations, a lively bar and restaurant, and three screens, the IFI was one of the first major cultural projects in Temple Bar. The programme focuses on cult and international film.

5 The Ark

There's a magical mini amphitheatre and lots of bright spaces for getting crafty at Europe's first custom-built children's cultural centre (suitable for kids aged 3–14). Irish and international artists have developed the fun programmes on offer, with the aim of extending horizons and stimulating the imagination. Kids can participate in exhibitions and theatrical workshops in this beautifully designed space.

7 Gallery of Photography

This contemporary space runs excellent exhibitions by Irish and international photographers. There are often photography courses and dark rooms to rent.

8 National Photographic Archive

This archive houses more than 300,000 photographs from the National Library. The changing exhibitions range from social and political history, to landscapes and postcards.

Regeneration

Sir William Temple bought this land for development in the 1600s and set about reclaiming the marshland to bring trade to the centre. The area thrived for a while, but with the development of the docks to the east, business began to decline. In the 1960s traders made use of the cheap rent and the area took on a Bohemian air. In the 1990s the government regenerated Temple Bar, creating the thriving entity it is today.

Christ Church Cathedral

The spectacularly imposing cathedral that we see today, towering over its surroundings, is largely a result of 19th-century restoration. Dublin's first church, made of wood, was founded here in 1028 by Sitric Silkenbeard, the first Christian king of the Dublin Norsemen. In 1172, however, Norman Richard de Clare, known as Strongbow, demolished the first church and commissioned his own stone version. The cathedral passed to the Protestant church during the Reformation and, together with St Patrick's Cathedral (see pp22–3), has remained in the use of the Church of Ireland. The huge crypt has been restored, with new floors and lighting.

Façade

🎵 Concerts are held in the main body of the cathedral and in the crypt, which is particularly atmospheric. Call for details.

• Christchurch Place
• Map D4
• 01-677 8099 • www. christchurchdublin.ie
• Open 9am–6pm Mon–Sat (7pm summer), 12:30–2:30pm and 4:30–6pm Sun (7pm summer); Closed 26 Dec; Last adm 30 mins before closing
• Partial dis. access
• Adm: cathedral, crypt & treasury €6. No photography in treasury
• Dublinia: Synod Hall; 01-679 4611; www.dublinia. ie; Open Mar–Sep: 10am–6.30pm daily, Oct–Feb: 10:30am–5:30pm Mon–Sat, 10am–4:30pm Sun; Dis. access; Adm €8.50 (combination tickets for Dublinia and cathedral available)

Top 10 Features

1 Great Nave
2 Strongbow's Tomb
3 Medieval Carvings
4 Crypt
5 Chapel of St Laud
6 Romanesque Doorway
7 Choir
8 Lord Mayor's Pew
9 Bridge to Synod Hall
10 Lady Chapel

Great Nave

The 25-m (80-ft) high nave *(below)* raises the spirits with its fine early Gothic arches. An example of the structural troubles that have beset the cathedral is visible on the north side, where the original 13th-century wall leans out by 50 cm (1.5 ft). This was a result of the collapse of the south wall in 1562.

Strongbow's Tomb

The tomb of the infamous Norman conqueror of Ireland *(above)* is a 16th-century replica and the effigy is not considered to be Strongbow, although it is possible that the fragment beside the tomb may be part of the original. Strongbow's remains are buried in the cathedral.

Medieval Carvings

Decorating the columns at the entrance to the North Transept, these 12th-century carvings depict two human faces enveloped by legendary griffons and a troupe of musicians. The middle pillar of the nave is adorned with fine gothic heads.

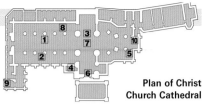

Plan of Christ Church Cathedral

Crypt
The vast crypt, the city's oldest structure, is unusual in that it runs the length of the building. It houses the treasury exhibition and a mummified cat *(above)* and rat.

Choir
At the centre of the church, the Victorian wooden stalls are set out for the choir. The Archbishop's Throne is set in pride of place.

Bridge to Synod Hall
This ornate Gothic bridge *(above)* was added during the rebuilding of the cathedral in the 1870s. Synod Hall is home to Dublinia, a well-presented re-creation of medieval Dublin *(see p56)*.

Lady Chapel
One of the other chapels opening off the central choir area is used to celebrate the daily Eucharist and provides a more intimate setting than the cathedral when numbers are small.

Chapel of St Laud
This chapel, one of three extending off the choir, is named after the 5th-century Normandy Bishop of Coutances. The chapel used to hold the preserved heart of Dublin's 12th-century patron saint, Laurence O' Toole. However, the heart was stolen in 2012 and has not been recovered.

Lord Mayor's Pew
Generally known as the Civic Pew, but historically belonging to the Lord Mayor, it is kept in the north aisle, but is moved to the front of the nave when required for ceremonial use. Decorated with a carving of the city, there is also a rest for the civic mace.

Strongbow
In the 12th century, the exiled king of Leinster, Dermot MacMurrough, looked to the Anglo-Normans for help to recover his kingdom. Richard de Clare, nicknamed Strongbow, answered the call and arrived in 1170 with his knights. He routed Leinster and conquered Dublin, then affirmed his loyalty to Henry II. It began centuries of English hold over Irish land.

Romanesque Doorway
This doorway *(right)*
is a fine example of 12th-century Irish stonework. The carvings on the capitals depict a musical troupe.

⭐🔟 St Patrick's Cathedral

St Patrick's, the Protestant Church of Ireland's national cathedral and commonly known as the "People's Cathedral", stands on an early Christian site where St Patrick is said to have baptized converts in a well in AD 450. Like Christ Church Cathedral (see pp20–21), the original structure was made of wood and it was not until 1190, when Archbishop John Comyn founded St Patrick's, that it was rebuilt in stone and its status raised to that of cathedral. The building has seen its fair share of politics: in 1649, during the Civil War, Cromwell's cavalry used it for stabling; not long after, Huguenot refugees from France sought solace here.

Façade

🎧 Choral evensong is held at 5:30pm Monday to Friday (3:15pm on Sunday). Sung Eucharist is at 11:15am on Sunday.

Services at Christmas and Easter can be very busy. Early arrival is advised.

• St Patrick's Close, Dublin 2
• Map D5
• 01-453 9472
• www.stpatrickscathedral.ie
• Open Mar–Oct: 9am–5:15pm daily; Nov–Feb: 9am–5pm Mon–Sat, 9am–2:30pm Sun
• Dis. access
• Adm €5.50 (students & seniors €4.20, family of four €15.00)

Top 10 Features

1. Minot Tower
2. Nave
3. Graves of Jonathan Swift and Stella
4. Boyle Monument
5. Lady Chapel
6. North Transept
7. South Transept
8. Choir
9. South Aisle
10. The Door of Reconciliation

Minot Tower
Believed to have been built for defence purposes, the almost 50-m (147-ft), 14th-century Minot Tower *(above)* still looks out of kilter with the rest of the cathedral.

Nave
St Patrick's is the longest medieval church in Ireland and the nave *(right)* reflects these immense proportions. The pillars are carved with an assortment of figures.

Graves of Jonathan Swift and Stella

One of the first ports of call for many visitors to the cathedral are the graves of Jonathan Swift *(see p34)* and his beloved Stella, positioned in the nave beneath brass tablets *(above right)*.

Lady Chapel
At the east end of the church, this 13th-century building was given over to the French Huguenots who arrived as refugees in the mid-17th century. They were given permission to worship here by the Dean and Chapter, and did so for almost 150 years.

North Transept
Hanging above the arches of the North Transept are a number of flags which commemorate Irish men and women who died in service of the British Army; some flags are up to 150 years old.

South Transept
This former Chapter House boasts a beautiful stained-glass window and, as with all areas of the cathedral, numerous monuments. Particularly interesting is that of Archbishop Marsh which has fine carvings by Grinling Gibbons.

Choir
Somewhat surprisingly, the choir *(centre)* is adorned with swords, banners and helmets above the pews. These represent the different knights of St Patrick who, until 1869, underwent their services of investiture in this chapel. Another memorial honours Duke Frederick Schomberg, slain during fighting at the Battle of the Boyne *(see p30)*.

Boyle Monument
The vast monument for the eminent Boyle family *(below)* is overrun with painted figures of the children of Richard Boyle, first Earl of Cork.

South Aisle
Memorials here honour renowned Irish Protestants of the 20th century. Douglas Hyde, Ireland's first president and founder of the Gaelic League is aptly remembered in Irish.

The Door of Reconciliation
A row between two 15th-century earls, Kildare and Ormond, reached stalemate when Ormond barricaded himself in the chapter house. Kildare cut a hole in the door *(below)* and offered to shake hands. From this incident came the expression "chancing your arm".

Jonathan Swift

Jonathan Swift was born in Dublin in 1667 and was educated at Trinity College *(see pp8–9)*. In 1694 he took holy orders and, after a year as a curate, moved to England as tutor to Esther Johnson at Moor Park in Surrey. Esther was to become the beloved "Stella" of his writings. Despite a reputation as a wit and pamphleteer, his ecclesiastical career was his primary concern and, in 1713, Swift was appointed dean of St Patrick's. On his death in 1745, he left a legacy of £8,000 to build St Patrick's Hospital for the Insane.

Top 10 Guinness Storehouse

Ask the majority of people what they most associate with Ireland, and the likelihood is the answer will be Guinness. Together with whiskey, it is the national drink, famous for its malty flavour and smooth, creamy head. Arthur Guinness founded this immensely successful business in 1759 from relatively humble beginnings but 250 years on, Guinness is the largest brewery in Europe and now the beer is available in more than 150 countries worldwide. The site at St James's Gate covers 55 acres and was unique for having its own water and electricity supply. This extraordinary exhibition covers all aspects of the production, with excellent displays and explanations, before a welcome free pint in one of the bars at the top of the building.

Brewery façade

🍽 The Brewer's Dining Hall serves quiche and pies as well as their signature beef and Guinness stew.

💡 Hold on to your perspex drop of Guinness given to you at the entrance – it is your ticket and a means to claim your free pint at the end.

The area around the Guinness Storehouse is quite isolated, so the Hop-on-Hop-off bus is a good option for getting there and back.

- St James's Gate, Dublin 8
- Map A5
- Bus No.123
- 01-408 4800
- www.guinness-storehouse.com
- Open 9:30am–5pm, daily; Jul–Aug: 9:30am–7pm
- Dis. access
- Adm €16.50 (students €13; children €6.50)

Top 10 Exhibits

1. Ingredients
2. Brewing Process
3. Arthur Guinness's Study
4. History of Cooperage
5. Transport Gallery
6. Advertising
7. Audiovisual
8. Guinness Abroad
9. Guinness at Home
10. Tasting

1 Ingredients
The tour logically begins with an interactive display about the process of selecting the right ingredients *(below)*. Barley, hops and yeast are displayed in huge barrels and there is a magnified area to see the ingredients close-up, accompanied by a pungent aroma.

2 Brewing Process
It takes a full ten days to brew the perfect pint of guinness. The roaster, kieve kettle, skimmer and maturation vessel are brought to life for visitors using 3D-animated graphics.

3 Arthur Guinness Room
Pictures of the chosen few *(below)* who have the palette of a master brewer are on display in this Guiness Hall of Fame, including Arthur and his son Arthur Guinness II.

History of Cooperage

Cooperage is the process of making and storing barrels (*above*). Films show how the coopers made the old wooden containers – metal casks have been used since the 1940s.

Advertising

Here TV and film advertising campaigns run on multi-split screens with the accompanying music, together with a display of all Guinness-associated products and posters (*below*).

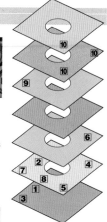

Plan of Guinness Storehouse

Guinness at Home

In this interactive exhibit, visitors are encouraged to write messages about their love of Guinness.

Tasting

Now is the time most visitors wait for – the free pint. There is a choice of three bars; the Gravity Bar (*above*) has magnificent views over the city.

Audiovisual

The legendary Irish *craic* – amusing tall stories told over a pint of the black stuff – is enjoyably illustrated in this feel-good audiovisual exhibit (*left*).

Transport Gallery

This display explains all methods of transporting Guinness to suppliers, from the old horse and cart to the sophisticated systems now operating worldwide.

Guinness Abroad

Figures are given that ten million glasses of Guinness are drunk in over 150 countries every day, and a huge glass panel shows what a good time everybody is having.

Arthur Guinness

Arthur Guinness (1725–1803) first bought a lease on a brewery in Leixlip in 1756. Three years later he gave this to his brother when he signed the lease for St James's Gate. He married Olivia Whitmore in 1761, and ten of their 21 children lived to establish a dynasty that has expanded into many activities worldwide.

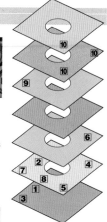

Kilmainham Gaol and Hospital

Despite their communal name, these two sights could not be more contrasting, both in their appearance and history. The forbidding gaol was built in 1796, but the material used was sandstone which wept in bad weather, resulting in damp and grim conditions that adversely affected the health of the inmates. The jail closed in 1924 and wasn't touched again until it was restored as a museum in the 1960s. Kilmainham Hospital, however, was built in the 1680s as one of Ireland's first Classical-style buildings – Sir William Robinson modelled the hospital on Les Invalides in Paris. It is now home to the Irish Museum of Modern Art (IMMA).

Kilmainham Gaol façade

An excellent café in the basement of the IMMA serves good vegetarian and organic dishes.

The hospital grounds are vast, with lovely views, so if the weather is good they are ideal for a picnic.

• Kilmainham Gaol: Inchicore Rd, Dublin 8; Map A4; 01-453 5984; Open Apr–Sep: 9:30am–6pm daily; Oct–Mar: 9:30am–5:30pm Mon–Sat, 10am–6pm Sun; Adm €6
• Kilmainham Hospital & IMMA: Royal Hospital, Military Rd, Dublin 8; Map A4; 01-612 9900; www.imma.ie; Open 11:30am–5:30pm Tue–Fri, 10am–5:30pm Sat, noon–5:30pm Sun; Dis. access; Free. Some rooms by guided tour only

Top 10 Features

1. Exhibition
2. West Wing
3. Gaol Chapel
4. East Wing
5. Tour
6. Kilmainham Gate
7. IMMA
8. Gardens and Courtyard
9. Great Hall
10. Hospital Chapel

Exhibition

Housed in a modern hall of the gaol, this exhibition puts visitors in the rather gruesome mood for what is to come. On the ground floor is a section on hanging techniques, while upstairs deals with the struggle for independence *(see p31)*.

West Wing

A fascinating if depressing place *(above)*, it doesn't take much to imagine the horror of internment here. The guide tells of the conditions the prisoners were subjected to – one hour of candlelight a night – and the types of hard labour.

Gaol Chapel

The most poignant story related about the chapel *(below)* is the wedding here of Joseph Plunkett and Grace Gifford. They married on the eve of Plunkett's execution, and were allowed 10 minutes alone together before Plunkett was taken out and shot.

For more historic buildings in Dublin See pp32–3

4 East Wing
A fine example of the "Panoptical" layout *(below)*, used in many Victorian prisons. The idea was to maximize light but allow for constant surveillance of the prisoners.

6 Kilmainham Gate
This austere doorway *(below)* is flanked by iron gates and sets the mood for a visit to the gaol. A long tree-lined avenue links the fine surroundings of the Kilmainham hospital to its much bleaker neighbour.

7 IMMA
Since its move here in 1991, the Irish Museum of Modern Art (IMMA) *(below)* has made full use of the space available. There is a regularly changing resident collection, so even the most regular visitor is likely to see something new. Innovative contemporary art features in touring exhibitions.

8 Gardens and Courtyard
The hospital's formal gardens *(left)*, designed between 1710 and 1720, were laid out in the French style with herbs and medicinal plants. They have been restored to their former glory.

9 Great Hall
This grand room served as the soldiers' dining room. The portraits of monarchs and viceroys, commissioned between 1690 and 1734, are the earliest surviving collection of institutional portraits in Ireland.

10 Hospital Chapel
The magnificent Baroque ceiling with its cherub heads and vegetable swags, was unlike anything seen in Ireland at that time. James Tabary, a Huguenot settler, carved the altar, reredos and rails from Irish oak in 1686.

5 Tour
A tour covering Irish history from 1796–1924 takes in a children's exercise yard and the Stone Breaker's Yard, in which the leaders of the 1916 uprising were executed by firing squad *(see p31).*

The History of Kilmainham Hospital

Kilmainham's Royal Hospital was built between 1680 and 1684 to the designs of Sir William Robinson, and is considered the most important 17th-century building in Ireland. Built for retired veterans, the hospital was handed over to the Free State in 1922 and served as the Garda headquarters from 1930–1950. It was one of the first buildings to benefit from Dublin's restoration programme in the 1980s. Beautifully renovated, it reopened in 1991 as the IMMA.

🔟 Phoenix Park

Surprisingly for such a small city, Phoenix Park is the largest enclosed urban park in Europe, covering an area of more than 1,750 acres. The name has no connection with the mythical bird but originates from the Gaelic Fionn Uisce which means "clear water" and refers to a spring that once existed here. Following the landscaping traditions of English parkland, complete with hundreds of deer, this is an idyllic place to escape from the bustling city centre. However, there's no shortage of things to do if you want to keep busy. At the weekends whole families spend the day here, indulging in a variety of activities from dog-walking to jogging, golf practice, hurling matches, charity runs, cricket and polo.

Phoenix Monument

🍺 Ryans, just out of the southeast gate in Parkgate Street, is one of the city's finest pubs both for drink and food.

🌳 Phoenix Park is not considered safe after dark.

• Phoenix Park: Park Gate, Conyngham Rd; www.phoenixpark.ie; Train: Heuston; Open daily; Free

• Visitor's Centre: 01-677 0095; Open Apr–Dec: 10am–6pm daily, Jan–Mar: 9.30am–5.30pm Wed–Sun; Partial dis. access; Free

• Zoo: 01-474 8900; www.dublinzoo.ie; Open Mar–Sep: 9:30am–6pm daily, Oct–Feb: 9:30am–dusk daily, last adm an hour before closing; Dis. access; Adm €16.50 (under-16s €11.80)

Top 10 Features

1. Áras an Uachtaráin
2. Phoenix Monument
3. Dublin Zoo
4. People's Garden
5. Papal Cross
6. Wellington Testimonial
7. Deerfield
8. Visitors' Centre
9. Ashtown Castle
10. Magazine Fort

1 Áras an Uachtaráin

This fine Palladian mansion (1751) by Nathaniel Clements was the viceregal lodge *(centre)*. In 1938 the lodge became the official home of the Irish president.

2 Phoenix Monument

The fourth Earl of Chesterfield erected this monument in 1747, topped with what has been described as a poor excuse for a phoenix, looking more like an eagle than the mythical bird.

3 Dublin Zoo

Dublin Zoo *(right)* dates back to 1831 – the second oldest in Europe. The Kaziranga Forest Trail is modelled on a region in India. It is home to a growing herd of Indian elephants.

4 People's Garden

Close to Park Gate and the police headquarters, this is the only formal area of the park. Decimus Burton landscaped the area in the 1830s and the effect is gentle and restful, as the landscaped hedges and flowerbeds merge with the wilder hillocks and ponds.

Papal Cross
The simplicity of the 35-m (116-ft) high stainless steel Papal Cross *(left)* is part of its beauty. It was erected on the spot where Pope John Paul II celebrated Mass in 1979, attended by more than a third of Ireland's population *(see p31)*.

Map of Phoenix Park

Magazine Fort
This former fort *(below)* became the main arms depot after independence, but it has been secured and abandoned since the IRA raid in 1939, when more than one million rounds of ammunition were stolen. It is now sadly decaying.

Wellington Testimonial
Designed by Robert Smirke as a testimonial to the Duke of Wellington, the monument *(right)* is the tallest in Europe at over 62 m (200 ft). It features four bronze plaques cast from cannons captured at Waterloo.

Deerfield
This beautiful 18th-century house was once the home of the British Chief Secretary for Ireland, Lord Cavendish, who was murdered in 1882 by an Irish nationalist. It is now the residence of the American ambassador.

Visitors' Centre
The display here shows the changing face of Phoenix Park, from 3500 BC to the present day. It also features a reconstruction of the Knockmaree Cist grave found in the park in 1838. On Saturday, free tours can be taken to Áras an Uachtaráin from here.

Ashtown Castle
A visit to this elegant tower house is included in the ticket to the Visitors' Centre. Its claim to fame is that it was once owned by the family of John Connell, an ancestor of Daniel O'Connell *(see p31)*. The tower was 'found' inside the walls of the 18th-century Ashtown Lodge when the lodge was due to be demolished.

The Development of Phoenix Park
In the 16th century, before the Reformation, the land at Phoenix Park belonged to the Knights Hospitallers of St John of Jerusalem. When the Dissolution of the Monasteries demanded the confiscation of all church lands, it became the property of the crown and the Duke of Ormond decided to enclose the land to provide a deer park for Charles II. In the mid-18th century much money was spent on developing Dublin City, including formalizing of the park. It was opened to the public in 1747.

Left **Pope John Paul II delivers mass in Phoenix Park** Right **Battle of the Boyne**

Moments in History

Newgrange
The first settlers arrived in Ireland from the Continent around 7000 BC, bringing with them farming skills and rudimentary tools which allowed them to establish small communities. The megalithic stone tomb of the Neolithic Age at Newgrange *(see p71)* is thought to date from around 3200 BC and is one of the most important passage graves in Europe.

Celts Arrive
Powerful tribes of warriors became established in Central Europe around 600 BC. With their ability to produce iron weapons and implements, the Celts were able to progress across the continent to Ireland. Earlier inhabitants remained, but the Celts (or Gaels) imposed their authority, culture and language.

Christianity Comes to Ireland
Although the Romans never settled in Ireland it was through them that Christianity reached Irish shores. The first bishop was appointed in AD 431 but it is

Stone tomb, Newgrange

St Patrick *(see p38)* who is credited with the conversion of the pagan Celts and the establishment of the Church between 432 and 461.

Viking Ireland
The Vikings arrived in Ireland in the AD 800 and established their own communities. In 1030 a wooden church was built where Christ Church Cathedral now stands *(see pp20–21)*.

First Irish Parliament
By the 1350s the Normans had settled in Ireland and introduced the feudal system of government, led by a justiciar who was head of the army, the chief judge and top administrator. He was helped in his work by a council of officials, and would occasionally summon a parliament consisting of his council, bishops, abbots and feudal lords. By the end of the 14th century, representatives of counties and towns were part of the process known as the Lower House, or Commons.

Battle of the Boyne
After his defeat by William of Orange at the Battle of the Boyne in 1690, James II fled to France leaving Ireland in the hands of the Protestant Ascendancy. These were English descendants of Tudor and Stuart settlers. The native Irish suffered for more than a century from the stringent penal measures inflicted on them.

For historic buildings in Dublin See pp32–3

7 Georgian High Culture

Many of the most important sights in the city, such as Custom House *(see p61)*, were built during the Georgian era. Artists and musicians visited Dublin from all over Europe – one of the highlights was the premiere of Handel's oratorio, *The Messiah*, in Dublin in 1741.

George Frederick Handel

8 The Great Famine

The potato famine dominated 19th-century Ireland. The crop failed first in 1845 as a result of potato blight. About two million people died of starvation or emigrated in desperation in a period that lasted until 1852.

9 The Easter Rising

On Easter Monday 1916 Patrick Pearse and others opposed to British rule proclaimed the Declaration of Independence from the General Post Office in O'Connell Street *(see p61)*. An uprising ensued and 15 insurgents were executed. In December 1921 the Anglo-Irish treaty was signed, creating the Irish Free State.

10 Pope John Paul II

In 1979 Pope John Paul II visited Ireland, the high point of which was his mass in Phoenix Park, attended by more than a million people. The Papal Cross marks the spot *(see p29)*.

Top 10 Politicians

1 Henry Grattan
Grattan (1746–1820) entered Parliament in 1775 and was a great champion of the Catholic cause.

2 Theobald Wolfe Tone
Tone (1763–98) has been described both as the founder of Irish nationalism and as a frustrated imperialist.

3 Daniel O'Connell
The greatest leader of Catholic Ireland, O'Connell (1775–1847) was a constant agitator against the Union.

4 Charles Stewart Parnell
Leader of the Irish Parliamentary Party in 1880, Parnell (1846–91) secured Gladstone's conversion to Home Rule.

5 Arthur Griffith
Griffith (1872–1922) launched Sinn Fein in 1906 and was elected president of the Dáil in 1922.

6 Patrick Pearse
Pearse (1879–1916) was executed for delivering the Proclamation of Independence in 1916.

7 Michael Collins
Commander-in-Chief of the government forces in the Civil War, Collins (1890–1922) was shot dead in his native County Cork.

8 Eamon de Valera
Valera (1882–1975) was President of the Republic from 1959–73. His political ideal was a 32-county Gaelic republic.

9 Charles Haughey
Prime minister for various terms from 1979 to 1992, Haughey (1925–2006) remains a controversial figure.

10 Mary Robinson
Mary Robinson was elected the first woman president in 1990.

Left **Custom House** Right **City Hall**

🔟 Historic Buildings

1 Dublin Castle

Originally rectangular in shape, Dublin Castle was designed as a "keepless castle", involving four circular corner towers and, midway along the south wall, a fifth tower. However, much of the medieval castle was destroyed by fire. The remodelling we see today began at the turn of the 18th century *(see pp14–17)*.

2 Custom House

James Gandon designed the striking Custom House in 1791. There are four decorated façades, with finely balanced end pavilions and recessed Doric columns facing the River Liffey. The exceptional statuary around the building is the work of Edward Smyth. A fire gutted the building in 1921 during the War of Independence, but it was restored in the same decade. The latest superb restoration work was carried out in the 1980s *(see p61)*.

3 Four Courts

West of Custom House is James Gandon's other magnificent edifice. Designed five years earlier in 1786, the Four Courts has a grand pedimented centre with arcaded screens and triumphal arches, topped with a colonnaded rotunda and a Neo-Classical dome. The five statues by Edward Smyth on the central block represent Moses, Wisdom, Authority, Justice and Mercy *(see p66)*.

4 City Hall

A competition was held in 1768 to select the designer of what was then to be the Royal Exchange, and Thomas Cooley's plans were the preferred choice. One of Dublin's most sophisticated Georgian buildings, it marked the introduction to Ireland of the Neo-Classical style of architecture, with its lofty dome supported by 12 columns and its 12 elegant circular windows *(see p54)*.

5 Leinster House

Designed by Richard Cassels in 1745, Leinster House is notable for its two contrasting façades, one resembling a town house, the other a country abode. Built for the Earl of Kildare, the building was acquired by the State in 1924.

Four Courts

Bank of Ireland
Built to accommodate the Irish House of Lords and House of Commons, the building is almost as magnificent as its English counterpart. Three architects were involved in its creation: Sir Edward Lovett Pearce designed the Palladian central block, with temple and portico flanked by colonnaded wings, in 1729; James Gandon contributed the portico to the east in 1785; and Richard Parkes added the western Ionic portico. In 1803, the building was taken over by the Bank of Ireland *(see p56)*.

Marsh's Library

Marsh's Library
Designed by Sir William Robinson of Kilmainham Hospital fame *(see pp26–7)* in 1701, this L-shaped library was built to house the collection of Archbishop Narcissus Marsh. The Gothic-style battlements and entrance date from the 19th century, but the oak bookcases, arranged in bays between the windows, are original. ◈ *St Patrick's Close • Map C5 • Open 9:30am–5pm Mon, Wed–Fri; 10am–5pm Sat • Adm*

Rotunda Hospital
Purpose-built as the first maternity hospital in Europe, founded by Dr Bartholomew Mosse in 1748, the building was designed by Richard Cassels. A number of other distinguished architects had a hand in the creation of the adjoining Assembly Rooms, which now comprise a cinema and the Gate Theatre *(see p63)*: John Ensor designed the rotunda in 1764, while the porches were added by Richard Johnston in 1784 and James Gandon in 1786 *(see p66)*.

Iveagh House
The first of architect Richard Cassels' notable Dublin houses, sadly the only part that now remains of the original is the first-floor saloon. Sir Benjamin Guinness linked two houses into one in the 1870s. His grandson, the second Lord Iveagh, later presented the house to the Irish Government. The building currently houses the Department of Foreign Affairs. ◈ *St Stephen's Green • Map F6 • Closed to the public*

Powerscourt Townhouse
This powerful looking building with its grand entrance was designed in 1771 by Robert Mack as a home for the third Viscount Powerscourt. The first-floor reception rooms, by Michael Stapleton, and the hall can still be appreciated even though the house was later converted into a shopping precinct *(see p55)*.

Powerscourt Townhouse

Left **Shaw's Birthplace** Centre **Oscar Wilde statue** Right **James Joyce statue**

Dublin Writers

1 James Joyce

The writer who most prolifically put Dublin on the literary map, Joyce (1882–1941) was born and educated in the city. He met Nora Barnacle on 16 June 1904 and, although they did not marry for 30 years, it became the date for events in his epic work *Ulysses*, published in Paris in 1922. *Dubliners* (1914), *Portrait of the Artist as a Young Man* (1916) and *Finnegan's Wake* (1939) are among his other works.

2 William Butler Yeats

Willliam Butler (1865–1939), brother of the painter Jack B Yeats, was born in Dublin. His first volume of poetry *The Wanderings of Oisin and Other Poems* was well received and later volumes confirmed his status as a leading poet. His play *On Baile's Strand* was chosen for the Abbey Theatre's opening in 1904 *(see p62)*.

3 George Bernard Shaw

Born in Dublin, Shaw (1856–1950) moved to England in 1876. Starting as a book reviewer for the *Pall Mall Gazette*, he was to become a prolific playwright; *The Devil's Disciple* (1897) and *Pygmalion* (1912) are just two of his works. He received the Nobel Prize for Literature in 1925.

4 Jonathan Swift

Swift (1667–1745) was born and educated in Dublin *(see p23)* and established a reputation as a wit through his satirical works. *A Modest Proposal* (1729), one of his most brilliant – if grim – satires, suggested feeding poor children to the rich. It is ironic that his work, *Gulliver's Travels* (1726), is a children's classic.

5 Oscar Wilde

Wilde (1854–1900) was born at Westland Row, Dublin, and became a classics scholar at Trinity College *(see pp8–9)* and later at Oxford. His highly popular plays, full of acid wit, include *An Ideal Husband* (1895) and *The Importance of Being Earnest* (1895). His imprisonment for homosexual offences inspired *The Ballad of Reading Gaol* (1898), but he died, destitute in Paris, in 1900.

6 Sean O'Casey

Dublin-born O'Casey (1880–1964) worked on the railways and became an active trades unionist. He achieved instant success with *The Shadow of a Gunman* (1923), set in the Dublin slums, followed by the play *Juno and the Paycock* in 1924 and his best-known work *The Plough and the Stars* in 1926. His later plays never had the appeal of the early works.

George Bernard Shaw bust

Samuel Beckett

Top 10 Contemporary Irish Writers

1 Seamus Heaney
Ireland's most prominent poet, Heaney (1939–2013) won the Nobel Prize for Literature in 1995. *North* (1975) explores the Troubles in Northern Ireland.

2 William Trevor
Trevor (b.1928) is a master of the short story genre.

3 John Banville
A screenwriter, Banville (b.1945) is also an award-winning novelist.

4 Anne Enright
Enright's (b. 1962) novel *The Gathering* (2007) won the prestigious Man Booker Prize.

5 Brian Friel
Playwright Friel's (b.1929) successes include *Dancing at Lughnasa* (1990).

6 Roddy Doyle
Renowned for his *Barrytown Trilogy* about Dublin life, Doyle (b.1958) won the Booker Prize in 1993 for *Paddy Clarke Ha Ha Ha*.

7 Edna O'Brien
The Country Girls (1960) is O'Brien's (b.1930) most well-known novel to date.

8 Colm Tóibín
Tóibín (b.1955) was shortlisted for the 2000 Booker Prize with his novel *Blackwater Lightship* (1999).

9 Frank McCourt
McCourt's (1930–2009) evocative account of a poverty-stricken upbringing in Limerick in *Angela's Ashes* (1996) won him the Pulitzer Prize.

10 Tom Murphy
A controversial playwright, Murphy's (b.1935) work *The Wake* (1998) had a long run at the Gate Theatre *(see p63)*.

7 Samuel Beckett
French Huguenot by descent, after a distinguished career at Trinity College, Beckett (1906–89) spent much of his life in France. The play *Waiting for Godot* (1952) made him an international name. He received the Nobel Prize for Literature in 1969.

8 John McGahern
Celebrated for his honest exploration of rural life in Ireland, McGahern (1934–2006) left the country after his early novel, *The Dark* (1965), was banned. He returned to country life in 1970 and lived on a farm until he died.

9 Elizabeth Bowen
Although born in Dublin, Elizabeth Bowen (1899–1973) spent much of her childhood in Cork. Her years in London are evoked in her novels, including *The Heat of the Day* (1949).

10 Patrick Kavanagh
Kavanagh (1904–67), born in Monaghan, went to London in 1939 and began a career as a poet and journalist. His reputation was established with a long and bitter poem of rural life, *The Great Hunger* (1942).

Left **Dublin Zoo** Right **Dublinia**

Children's Attractions

The Ark
Workshops, art classes, plays, exhibitions and concerts geared towards children between two and 12 years. Book ahead.
⊛ *11a Eustace St • Map E4 • 01-670 7788 • Open daily • www.ark.ie • Adm*

Dublinia
Medieval Dublin is brought to life, through exhibits such as a full-size reconstruction of a merchant's house *(see p56)*.

Dublin Zoo
Apart from the usual exotic animals there is a petting zoo, playgrounds, and a train ride *(see pp28–9)*. ⊛ *01-474 8900*

My Museum
An exciting programme of activities run by the National Museum of Ireland, which rotates between the city's museums.
⊛ *01-677 7444 • Sun pm • www.museum.ie*

Viking Splash Tour
A costumed driver gives a lively tour on land in a military amphibious vehicle before splashing into the waters of the Grand Canal Quay. Passengers are encouraged to let out Viking roars. ⊛ *Stephen's Green • Map F5 • Open mid-Feb–Nov: daily • Adm*

National Wax Museum
Kids will enjoy the "Children's Fantasy World", the Chambers of Horrors and models of pop idols.
⊛ *Foster Place • Map E4 • 01-671 8373 • Open 10am–7pm Mon–Sat • Adm*

Science Gallery
Science meets art at this innovative museum located in Trinity College. Exhibitions change regularly. ⊛ *01-896 4091 • Map N5 • Open noon–8pm Tue–Fri, noon–6pm Sat & Sun • www.sciencegallery.com • Free*

Sea Safari
An exhilirating excursion for children aged eight and over. Take a trip around the headland in a rigid inflatable boat, including a trip to Dalkey Island.
⊛ *Poolbeg Marina • 01-668 9802 • Tours by appointment only • www.seasafari.ie*

Lambert Puppet Theatre
Classic pantomime fun; performances range from fairy tales for toddlers to Yeats for older kids. ⊛ *Clifton Lane, Monkstown • Dart Salthill • 01-280 0974 • Open Sat & Sun • www.lambertpuppettheatre.ie • Adm*

Gotham Café
A fun café-restaurant serving pizzas and more for hungry little visitors *(see p59)*. ⊛ *01-670 5266*

Left **Dublin Horse Show** Right **Six Nations Rugby**

🔟 Sporting Events

Dublin Horse Show
The Fáilte Ireland Dublin Horse Show is one of the world's top international equestrian events. The event takes place over five days, and includes a hotly contested Ladies' Day. It attracts more than 20,000 spectators. ✪ *RDS, Ballsbridge • Dart Sandymount • Early Aug*

Six Nations Rugby
The Aviva Stadium at Lansdowne Road plays host as the Irish venue for this competition. ✪ *Lansdowne Road • Jan–Mar*

Leopardstown Christmas Racing Festival
Events occur year round at Leopardstown, but the four-day Christmas Racing Festival is one of the highlights of the Irish racing calendar. Built in 1888, the course offers some of the finest hospitality suites in racing. ✪ *Leopardstown • 26–29 Dec*

Fairyhouse Racing Festival
Every Easter the historic Fairyhouse racing course hosts the Irish Grand National. ✪ *Fairyhouse • Easter weekend*

Dublin Marathon
Winding through the historic streets of the city, the Dublin Marathon attracts thousands of participants and spectators. ✪ *Last Mon in Oct*

All-Ireland Hurling Final
The world's oldest field sport requires a huge amount of skill to control a speeding ball (*sliotar*) with a hurl made of ash. The fastest field sport in the world, expect lots of excitement and a bit of blood. ✪ *Croke Park • Train Heuston • First Sun in Sep*

All-Ireland Football Final
Gaelic football is similar to Aussie football. The pace is the same and allows carrying of the ball. The goals are divided between the net area, similar to soccer (three points), as well as rising posts (one point). ✪ *Croke Park • Train Heuston • Third Sun in Sep*

Laytown Races
The only Irish horse race run on a beach. As the tide rolls out, the finishing posts rise and bookies open shop. ✪ *Laytown • Train Connolly • Sep*

Women's Mini Marathon
With over 40,000 participants, this 10-km (6-mile) race is one of the largest all-female sporting events in the world. ✪ *First Mon in Jun*

Colours Boat Race
Crowds flock to the Liffey as Trinity and University College Dublin compete in the age-old rivalry of a rowing race between O'Connell Bridge and St James's Gate, The tiny Ha'penny Bridge *(see p56)* fills with spectators. ✪ *First Sat in Apr*

Above **Details from a stained-glass window, depicting Irish legends**

:10 Irish Legends and Myths

1 St Patrick

Patrick, a 5th-century Roman Briton, was captured by Irish raiders and taken into slavery in Ulster. Escaping back to Britain, he became a priest and returned to Ireland to help convert the Irish. Extraordinary tales about him abound – he cured the sick, raised the dead, and rid Ireland of snakes by ringing his bell *(see p30)*.

2 The Children of Lir

The greatest of the *Tuatha dé Danann*, or fairy folk, was the sea-god Lir. His four beloved children were turned into swans by their jealous stepmother Aoife, who condemned them to live forever in the waters off the Ulster coast. Some 900 years later, a Christian named Caomhog broke the spell, baptizing them as they died.

3 Punishment of the Children of Tuireann

For murdering his father, the sun god Lugh demanded that the three sons of Tuireann give him magical objects and perform difficult feats. Their last task was to make three shouts from the Hill of Miochaoin.

4 Cúchulainn

The boy Setanta had miraculous strength and loved the game of hurling. Invited to a feast by the legendary black-smith Culain, Setanta arrived late and was met by the smith's ferocious guard dog. He killed the hound with his hurley stick and offered himself as a guard instead. He was renamed Cúchulainn, "hound of Culain".

5 Oisin in Tír na nÓg

Fionn mac Cumhaill's son Oisin and Niamh, daughter of sea-god Manannan, went together to Tír na nÓg, paradise of eternal youth. After 300 years, homesick Oisin borrowed Niamh's magic horse to revisit Ireland. His feet were not to touch the ground, but he fell from the horse, instantly aged 300 years and died.

6 Deirdre and the Exile of the Sons of Usnach

King Conchubar loved Deirdre, his harpist's beautiful daughter. The Druid Cathbad foretold she would bring disaster, so her father Fedlimid kept her in solitude. But Deirdre loved young

Cúchulainn

Discover more at **www.traveldk.com**

Naoise, son of Usnach, who, with his brothers, took her to Scotland. After persuading them to return, Conchubar killed Usnach's sons. Deirdre, grief-stricken, killed herself.

Cattle Raid of Cooley

Connacht's Queen Medb (Maeve) raided Ulster to seize the chief Daire's famous bull. All the men of Ulster being under a spell, the boy Cúchulainn fought alone, killing all Medb's warriors. Medb retreated.

Pursuit of Diarmaid and Grainne

Fionn mac Cumhaill asked King Cormac for the hand of his daughter Grainne, but she eloped with Fionn's nephew Diarmaid. For a year and a day Diarmaid and Grainne fled as enraged Finn pursued them around Ireland.

Fionn and the Salmon of Knowledge

The first person to taste the Salmon of Knowledge would gain prophetic powers. When the young Fionn mac Cumhaill – hero of countless legends – visited Finnegas, the old druid caught the fish. While it cooked, Fionn's thumb touched the salmon. Putting the thumb to his lips, he tasted the fish before Finnegas.

Destruction of Dinn Ríg

Cobthach of Bregia killed his brother Lóegaire, the King of Leinster. Some legends say that Lóegaire's grandson, Moen, was spared, but was made to drink of his grandfather's blood and was struck dumb. Later, Moen miraculously recovered his speech and was renamed Labraid ("speaks"). He eventually killed Cobthach by locking him in a house and burning him to death.

Top 10 Celtic Traditions

1 Celtic Crosses
High, richly carved stone crucifixes with a central circle are a feature of Celtic churches.

2 Celtic Design
Distinctive traditional interlocking patterns that decorate ancient Celtic jewellery have always remained popular in Ireland.

3 Language
The Irish language, spoken by about 1.7 million people today, comes directly from the ancient Celtic inhabitants.

4 Céilí
A get-together to drink, sing, dance and stamp your feet to traditional music.

5 Hurling
This robust Celtic game requires hurleys (ash sticks), a *sliotar* (a leather ball) and plenty of energy.

6 Musical Instruments
Uillean pipes, *bodhráns* (drums), tin whistles and other Celtic instruments remain at the heart of Irish folk music.

7 St Brigid's Crosses
Country people still weave rushes into these crosses and hang them up to protect against evil spirits.

8 Fairy Trees
An isolated tree in a field is generally not cut down because it could be sacred.

9 Water Worship
Sacred springs, fairy wells, and holy water remain a large part of many Irish people's religion.

10 Craic
The lively, witty, relaxed conviviality, gossip and talk that makes life worth living.

Left **Gaiety Theatre** Right **Gate Theatre**

🔟 Performing Arts Venues

1 National Concert Hall
For quality classical music, look no further: it is Dublin's premier venue, hosting guests of the calibre of the New York Philharmonic. The building is also home to Ireland's National Symphony Orchestra. Jazz, contemporary and traditional Irish music are also performed here, and there are lunchtime concerts in summer. ❧ *Earlsfort Terrace • 01-417 0000 • Map F6 • Dis. access*

2 The Abbey and Peacock Theatres
The Abbey is a legend. Founded in the early 20th century by a circle of writers including the poet WB Yeats, it gained renown at the cutting edge of Irish theatre. Controversial works by new writers such as Sean O'Casey and JM Synge were staged here, the latter causing riots on opening night. Now classics, these are the mainstay of the Abbey. Experimental work is shown in the sister theatre, the Peacock *(see p62)*. ❧ *01-878 7222 (Abbey)*

3 The Gate Theatre
Since its founding in 1928, the Gate has been one of the most daring theatres in Europe, introducing Irish audiences to Ibsen and Chekhov and producing Oscar Wilde's *Salome* while it was banned in England. Orson Welles and James Mason began their acting careers here. Go early for a pre-performance drink in the cosy bar *(see p63)*. ❧ *01-874 4045*

4 The Gaiety Theatre
Dublin's oldest theatre dates from 1871. The gilded auditorium is an atmospheric backdrop for a wide range of entertainment, but, as its name suggests, the Gaiety leans more towards music and comedy. ❧ *S King St • Box office: 01-679 5622 • Map E5 • Dis. access*

5 The Olympia Theatre
Opened in 1878 as a music hall, after years of rivalry with the Gaiety the Olympia settled down to staging a similar gamut of musicals and comedy. ❧ *Dame St • Box office: 01-679 3323 • Map E4*

6 Bewley's Café Theatre
This is a unique opportunity for lunchtime drama from Monday to Saturday on the second floor of Bewley's on Grafton Street. There are evening events also such as cabaret and jazz. ❧ *78/79 Grafton St • 086-878 4001 • Map E4*

Gaiety Theatre foyer

Olympia Theatre

Project Arts Centre
Born as a spin-off project to the Gate, the Project is perhaps the most vibrant centre of performance art in the city, with young companies exploring innovative dance, music, drama and poetry. U2, Liam Neeson and Gabriel Byrne were all rising stars here. ◈ 39 E Essex St • 01-881 9613 • Map E3 • Dis. access

Samuel Beckett Theatre
This theatre was opened in 1992 to celebrate the quatercentenary of Trinity College. During term it showcases the work of the department. At other times it hosts prestigious Irish and international companies.
◈ Trinity College • 01-896 2461 • Map F4

Bord Gais Energy Theatre
This diamond in the Docklands is a fantastic venue for West End touring productions, opera, ballet, theatre and popular music.
◈ Grand Canal Square, Docklands • 01-677 7999 • Map D4 • Dis. access

The Helix
This glass and granite building at Dublin City University has an excellent reputation for diverse theatre, opera and music productions. ◈ Collins Ave, DCU, Glasnevin • 01-700 7000 • Dis. access

Top 10 Cultural Events

Dublin Theatre Festival
This two-week event showcases a wealth of Irish talent. ◈ 44 E Essex St • 01-677 8439 • Map E3 • Late Sep–Oct

St Patrick's Festival
A week-long series of events surrounds the parade on the day. ◈ 17 Mar

Wexford Opera Festival
Performances of three different operas at Wexford Opera House, supported by daytime fairs. ◈ Map P5 • Oct

Galway International Arts Festival
Massive celebration of film, theatre, art, literature and music. ◈ Map N2 • Jul–Aug

Bloomsday
Fans of James Joyce re-enact his novel *Ulysses* on the day it is set. ◈ 16 Jun

Dublin International Film Festival (DIFF)
The best of Irish and worldwide cinema. ◈ Spring

Great Music in Irish Houses Festival
Chamber music events in mansions around Ireland. ◈ Jun

Cork Jazz Festival
An extremely popular festival with performances and events throughout the city. ◈ End Oct

Dublin Fringe Festival
The Fringe includes dance, street performances, visual arts and comedy. ◈ 2 weeks in Sep

Temple Bar TradFest
Staged over five days and with over 200 events, this is Dublin's biggest Irish music and culture festival. ◈ Temple Bar • 01-703 0700 • Map E4 • Jan

Left **Mulligans** Right **The Long Hall**

🔟 Pubs

Kehoe's
Just off Grafton Street, this cosy pub has lost none of its original character. It's usually busy, but there's a large snug to hide away in, just beside the entrance. Close to Trinity College, it has a good mix of students and old pub characters. ◈ *9 S Anne St • F5*

Ryan's
This beautifully preserved pub has self-contained snugs – originally for "the ladies" – on each side of the counter. The decor is Victorian in every detail, from the mahogany partitions and sepia photographs to the brass match lighters fixed to the counter. Upstairs is a cosy restaurant which has won several awards. ◈ *Parkgate St • Train Heuston*

Mulligans
Once a working-class drinking man's pub (there were originally no chairs, since "real men" should stand as they

drank), Mulligan's has since attracted a mixed bag, including former US President John F Kennedy. It is still stark, but cosy nonetheless, and constantly busy. For literature buffs, it features in the writings of James Joyce. Perhaps the best Guinness in Dublin: try a pint and cast your vote. ◈ *8 Poolbeg St • F3*

The Stag's Head
Built in 1770, the Stag's Head was refurbished in the opulent Victorian style, resembling a mix between a church and a mansion, with bottle-glass windows, mirrors reaching up to the high ceiling, a counter topped with Connemara marble, plus, of course, the scary antlered namesake on the wall. James Joyce also drank here, and it has featured in many films. A magnet for students, it tends to get lively. Good pub grub. ◈ *1 Dame Court, off Dame St • Map E4*

Neary's
This cosy Edwardian-style pub, backing onto the Gaiety Theatre *(see p40)*, is frequented by theatrical types. Actor Peter O'Toole and writer Flann O'Brien famously used to have a tipple or two here too. ◈ *1 Chatham St • Map E5*

Pub sign, The Stag's Head

The Long Hall

Backing onto Dublin Castle, this is very much a locals' pub, although many visitors come to experience its evocative atmosphere. The decor includes chandeliers and a pendulum clock more than 200 years old. *51 S Great George's St • Map D4*

O'Donoghue's

Music and fun are the lifeblood of this pub, which fostered the popular balladiers, The Dubliners. Tap your feet on the Liscannor stone floor during an informal music session, or, if the sun's shining, have a drink in the little courtyard out back. *15 Merrion Row • Map F6 • Dis. access*

The Brazen Head

This pub, in the heart of Viking Dublin, is the oldest in the in the country, dating back to 1198. It has served a colourful set of patriots, including James Joyce, Brendan Behan, Van Morrison and Garth Brooks. The courtyard is a lovely spot for trying out one of the best pints of Guinness in Dublin and listening to traditional music. *20 Lower Bridge St • Map C4 • Dis. access*

O'Donoghue's

Café en Seine

Decorated in French coffeehouse style, the three floors of this large café-bar are filled with giant lampshades, huge mirrors, ornate sculptures and plants stretching up to a roof-height glass atrium. Expect to queue on weekend nights. *40 Dawson St • Map F5*

The Porterhouse

Dublin's very own brewing company, located in Temple Bar, the city's busy cultural quarter. Try one of the ten beers brewed on the premises, such as a "pint of Plain" porter, Oyster stout (made with fresh oysters) or Temple Braü pilsner. There is tasty food and plenty of live music too. *16 Parliament St • Map D4*

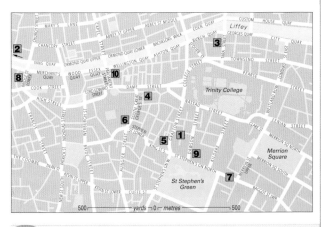

Left **Lillie's Bordello** Right **The International Bar**

Nightspots

The International Bar
You'd be content if this was just a watering hole – wood panelling and a healthy tradition make this one of the best drinking spots in town. Things get even better on music nights when bands play blues and soul upstairs. Tuesdays and Thursdays are jazz nights and host some of Dublin's best talent. Comedy shows all week *(see p58)*. ◈ *01-677 9250*

The Workman's Club
The deep-red walls and well-worn wooden floors of this live music venue radiate rock 'n' roll. Home to the original Dublin Workingmen's Club from 1888 until 2003, this labyrinthine club is a quayside gem. It boasts perhaps the best rooftop bar in the city along with the coolest crowds. ◈ *10 Wellington Quay • 01-670 6692 • Map D4*

Whelan's

Copper Face Jack's
This lively and popular nightclub is known to Dubliners as Coppers and attracts a young, thoroughly unpretentious and fun-loving crowd. The DJs play chart music late into the night, all week long. ◈ *29-30 Harcourt St • 01-475 8777 • Map E6*

The Grand Social
With its packed programme of comedy, clubbing, bands and flea markets, The Grand Social is arty, eclectic and fun. Quirky features include a vending machine full of guitar strings and kazoos. The top floor has a circus vibe and the carnival atmosphere spills on to the street. ◈ *35 Lower Liffey St • 01-874 0076 • Map E3*

Lillie's Bordello
Not the place to chill out and have a pint of the black stuff, but nothing about Lillie's Bordello is traditional. You need to be a trend-setter to get through the door and celebrities frequent the private, reserved suites. Commoners compete to be seen and good music ties it together. ◈ *Adam Court, Grafton St • 01-679 9204 • Map F4*

The Button Factory
One of the best live music venues in the city with an exciting line-up of international and local bands. Club nights are Thursday to Sunday. They also have a varied calendar of dance and theatre events. ◈ *Curved St, Temple Bar • 01-670 9202 • Map E4*

The Sugar Club

The Sugar Club
In what used to be a cinema, the crowd comes for the cocktail bar and performances – everything from casino nights and salsa to the "next big thing". ◈ *8 Lower Leeson St • 01-678 7188 • Map E5*

The Academy
Four thumping floors of music to cater for most tastes from big-draw acts to smaller gigs and also comedy shows. Late-night club Wednesday to Sunday. ◈ *57 Middle Abbey St • 01-877 9999 • Map E3*

Rí-Rá
Gaelic for "uproar", the Rí-Rá is a relaxed yet vibrant club playing a mix of R&B, hip hop, soul, disco and electro. The fashionable Globe bar upstairs serves snacks during the day. ◈ *11 S Great George's St • 01-671 1220 • Map E4*

Whelan's
It looks like your average pub, but walk through the bar to the back and you'll find one of Dublin's most happening live venues. ◈ *25 Wexford St • 01-478 0766 • Map D6*

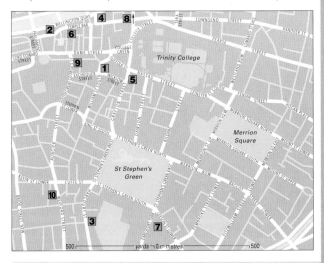

Left **Bewley's, Grafton Street** Right **Moore Street Market**

Shopping Areas

Grafton Street
Probably the most famous pedestrian thoroughfare in Dublin, Grafton Street traditionally caters to up-market shoppers, with homegrown department stores such as Brown Thomas *(see p57)* and Weir's, Dublin's largest and most exclusive jewellers. Buskers offer a lively atmosphere.

Powerscourt Townhouse
Irish designer labels and antiques shops cluster around the indoor courtyard of this 18th-century converted town house. Products range from handmade jigsaw puzzles to antique jewellery and Irish silver. The Design Centre is upstairs, with the cream of Irish fashion. When you've had enough, there are plenty of cafés and bars here too *(see p55)*.

Grafton Street

Henry Street
Henry Street is lively and buzzing along its pedestrian route, while Moore Street's outdoor food market adds colour to the proceedings. Shops and department stores here tend to be better value than those south of the river. Arnotts department store is one of the most attractive in the city. ◈ *Map E2*

St Stephen's Green Shopping Centre
This delicate masterpiece of glass and light is a pleasant place to shop, with Irish department store Dunnes Stores, as well as international fashions from TK Maxx, Benetton and Quicksilver. There's a selection of cafés, with great views of St Stephen's Green. ◈ *St Stephen's Green • Map F6 • Dis. access*

Francis Street
Dublin is one of Europe's best cities for antiques, and Francis Street and the surrounding area are an antique-hunter's dream, lined with deliciously dusty shops. Beware: the attitude may be relaxed, but the goods don't come cheap. ◈ *Map C4*

Jervis Street Shopping Centre
This large modern shopping centre contains shops selling food, household goods, fashion and sports gear. British chains such as Boots and Argos cater for most consumer needs. ◈ *1A Jervis St • Map E3 • Dis. access*

George's Street Arcade

Top 10 Food Sellers

1 Epicurean Food Hall
A mouthwatering display of international favourites, from Mexican *burritos* to Greek salads. ✪ *1 Liffey St • Map F2*

2 Temple Bar Market
The sale of farmhouse cheeses, organic vegetables and similar is soundtracked by street musicians. Saturday only. ✪ *Meeting House Sq • Map E3*

3 Moore Street Market
Last-chance bargains on vegetables, flowers and other produce. ✪ *Map E2*

4 Dunne & Crescenzi
Selling more than 100 Italian wines, fine olive oil and artisan products. ✪ *S Frederick St • Map F5*

5 Sheridans Cheesemongers
The best in Irish farmhouse cheese. ✪ *11 S Anne St • Map F5*

6 Butlers Chocolate Café
Dublin's own chocolate brand, founded on Lad Lane in 1932. ✪ *24 Wicklow St • Map E4*

7 Fallon & Byrne
All kinds of speciality ingredients are sold at this New York-style food hall. ✪ *Exchequer St • Map E4*

8 Listons
More than 4,000 gourmet products are available here. ✪ *25–26 Lower Camden St • Map E6*

9 Terroirs
Fine wines and gourmet food sold in this elegant shop. ✪ *103 Morehampton Rd, Donneybrook • Bus No. 10*

10 Avoca Food Hall
Foodstuffs from around the world and Irish crafts in the basement. ✪ *11–13 Suffolk St • Map D2*

7 Blackrock Market
A quick trip on the DART will take you out to the seaside village of Blackrock where, at weekends, an 18th-century tavern and courtyard house more than 60 stalls selling second-hand books, clothes and bric-à-brac, as well as genuine antiques. ✪ *Main St, Blackrock • Dis. access*

8 Liberty Market
Ideal for bargain-hunting, this market sells mainly fresh food and domestic goods. It's worth coming here just to soak up the atmosphere of one of the oldest areas of the city. ✪ *Meath & Thomas Sts • Map B4 • Thu–Sat*

9 George's Street Arcade
This lovely redbrick market has established shops on either side, with stalls down the centre. Exotic fruits rub shoulders with New Age baubles, fortune-tellers and vintage clothing. ✪ *S Great George's St • Map E5*

10 Westbury Mall
This covered walkway with boutiques and up-market cafés is a good place to escape a sudden downpour – all too common in Dublin. ✪ *Balfe St • Map E5*

Left **Patrick Guilbaud** Right **The Lobster Pot**

🔟 Restaurants

Patrick Guilbaud
The only two-star Michelin restaurant in Ireland. It offers "modern classic cuisine using Irish produce in season". Guilbaud uses Ireland's bountiful fresh fish, meat and game to create savoury Gallic dishes. The restaurant is set in one of the brick town houses that make up The Merrion hotel *(see p128)*. Furnished in 18th-century style, it makes a great setting for this timeless cuisine. ⓢ *21 Upper Merrion St • Map G5 • 01-676 4192 • Dis. access • €€€€€*

Chapter One
The arched granite walls of the basement of the Dublin Writer's Museum are home to one of the city's finest restaurants. Here they serve superb authentic Irish cooking with classic French cuisine influences. The menu varies according to the seasonally available locally grown organic produce. There's an excellent charcuterie trolley. There is also a popular two-course, pre-theatre menu *(see p67)*.

Chapter One

Pichet
The ever-popular Pichet promises a really special yet unpretentious dining experience. The chic decor and lively atmosphere provide a perfect setting to enjoy classic dishes such as suckling pig. The indulgent Hereford rib-eye steak béarnaise is a firm favourite. ⓢ *14–15 Trinity St • Map E4 • 01-677 1060 • €*

101 Talbot
A reputation for excellent, creative dishes at reasonable prices have helped 101 Talbot to become one of the north city's most popular restaurants. Menus mix a variety of local, European and Middle Eastern influences *(see p67)*.

The Lobster Pot
A seafood restaurant set in a redbrick terrace house, the service and the cuisine are delightfully old-fashioned. As the name suggests, the chef uses as much fresh Irish sea catch as possible to produce favourites such as Kilmore crab and prawn bisque. ⓢ *9 Ballsbridge Terrace • Train Lansdowne Road • 01-668 0025 • €€€*

L'Gueuleton
This packed French-style bistro serves delicious yet reasonably priced food. Try a dozen *petit gris escargots* to start, move on to dry aged beef cheek with an oxtail croquette or slow roast pork belly with Jack

McCarthy's black pudding for the next course and end with banana tarte tatin. They don't take bookings so arrive early.
🖎 1 Fade St • Map E5 • 01-675 3708 • Limited dis. access • €€€

L'Ecrivain
Five minutes' walk from St Stephen's Green, this extremely popular award-winning restaurant creates original masterpieces from French-inspired dishes, accompanied by wines worthy of the food. Chef Derry Clarke and his team use fresh Irish ingredients to work the magic. Worth the price. Book ahead.
🖎 190A Lower Baggot St • Map G6 • 01-661 1919 • Closed Sat lunch, Sun • Dis. access • €€€€

Cleaver East
One of the city's most talked about eateries, Cleaver East is located at the city centre. It serves up delicious sharing plates such as lobster dumplings, oriental mushrooms and lemongrass broth, and cushion of venison with braised red cabbage and wild mushrooms. The decor alone is worth a visit.
🖎 East Essex St, Temple Bar, Dublin 2 • Map E4 • 01-531 3500 • Dis. access • €

Chez Max
This gorgeous little French restaurant, Chez Max, will never be out of fashion. Tucked away in the small lane beneath the Dublin Castle, this intimate venue serves a menu of rich and simple cuisine by candlelight. The outdoor tables overlooking the castle entrance are perfect

Trocadero

for a morning espresso and there is a heated garden at the back for alfresco evening dining. You can find its more spacious twin at 133 Lower Baggot Street. 🖎 1 Palace St • Map D4 • 01-633 7215 • €

Trocadero
Held in high esteem by locals and visitors alike, Trocadero is the archetypal Dublin theatre restaurant. The decor offers much to talk about with many famous stage personalities gazing down from its dark walls. Choose the excellent steak and stay late to soak up the incredible atmosphere here. 🖎 4 St Andrew's St • Map E4 • 01-677 5545 • €€€

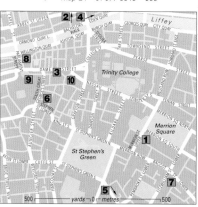

AROUND TOWN

South of the Liffey
52–59

North of the Liffey
60–67

Greater Dublin
68–77

DUBLIN'S TOP 10

Left **Trinity College** Right **St Patrick's Cathedral**

South of the Liffey

DUBLIN TAKES ITS NAME FROM THE SOUTHWEST OF THE CITY *when, in prehistoric times, there was a dark pool (Dubh Linn) at the confluence of the River Liffey and what was once the River Poddle. The area expanded during the 18th century, when the cobbled streets of Temple Bar became a centre for merchants and craftsmen – interestingly reverting to similar use in the 20th century. Prior to the founding of Trinity College in 1592, southeast Dublin was relatively undeveloped. St Stephen's Green wasn't enclosed until the 1660s and it remained for private use until 1877. But from the 1850s the area witnessed a boom that saw the construction of important public buildings such as City Hall. Today, the south is the hub of the fashionable scene, with designer stores and fine restaurants.*

Christ Church Cathedral

🔟 Sights

1. Trinity College
2. National Museum
3. National Gallery
4. Dublin Castle
5. Temple Bar
6. Christ Church Cathedral
7. St Patrick's Cathedral
8. City Hall
9. Grafton Street
10. Powerscourt Townhouse

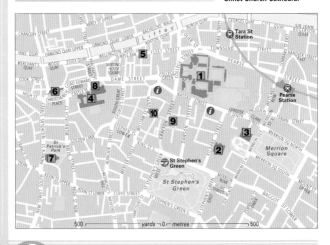

National Museum

Trinity College
Ireland's premier institute of education was founded in 1592 by Queen Elizabeth I on the site of an Augustinian monastery. A Protestant-only college at its start, Trinity did open its doors to Catholic students in 1793, but it wasn't until the 1970s that the Catholic Church relaxed its opposition to the college. Its quadrangles are peaceful havens, and its priceless *Book of Kells* a highlight *(see pp8–9)*.

National Museum of Ireland
Only two of the museum's three sites are south of the river: the Natural History Museum *(see p56)* and the branch on Kildare Street which examines Irish archaeology and history. The latter's 19th-century building is almost as impressive as its collections, decorated with marble and mosaics *(see pp10–11)*.

National Gallery of Ireland
An expansion to the gallery on Clare Street has vastly increased the space available for temporary exhibitions and displays of the gallery's permanent collection. The improved facilities also include a large shop, a café and restaurant and a number of lecture theatres *(see pp12–13)*.

Dublin Castle
Built into the city walls in 1204, the castle was Dublin's greatest stronghold, designed to defend the British-ruled city against the native Irish. It was at that time protected by rivers on both sides, the Liffey to the north and the Poddle to the south. The castle was completely reconstructed after a fire in 1684 and was further refined during the Georgian period, from which time most of the ornate state apartments date *(see pp14–17)*.

Temple Bar
This hugely popular area is the heart of south Dublin and has a seemingly limitless array of cafés, restaurants and bars as well as interesting little shops and cultural centres. On the banks of the Liffey, the term "bar" meant a riverside path. Its bustling atmosphere and trendy businesses, residents and clientele are the personification of Dublin's emergence as one of Europe's most successful, fashionable and popular cities *(see pp18–19)*.

Temple Bar

Christ Church Cathedral

One of the city's two great cathedrals, illustrating the importance religion has always played in Dublin life, Christ Church was the first to be built, in 1038. Although nothing of the original wooden church now stands, there are plenty of beautiful medieval features and decorations to appreciate, including floor tiles and stone carvings. The "Treasures of Christ Church" exhibition, housed in the 12th-century crypt, includes a gilt plate donated by William III in 1697 (see pp20–21).

St Patrick's Cathedral

Dublin's "second" cathedral and long-time rival to Christ Church. Apart from the many monuments and plaques com-memorating deceased dignitaries, and some fine architectural features, St Patrick's most interesting association is with Jonathan Swift. Appointed dean at the beginning of the 18th century, Swift carried out much of his work from the cathedral. You can see his death mask, writing desk and chair in the north pulpit and the memorial to himself and "Stella" lies just inside the entrance (see pp22–3).

City Hall

Thomas Cooley designed this stately building between 1769 and 1779. He had won the commission as a result of a competition, beating his better-known contemporary James Gandon who designed the Four Courts and Custom House (see p61). Cooley made a fine job of City Hall, which was originally built as the city's Royal Exchange. City bureaucrats latterly used it for various purposes but, having undergone extensive restoration, it is now open to the public. There is an excellent permanent exhibition in the reconstructed vaults entitled "The Story of the Capital", covering 1,000 years of Dublin's fascinating history.
Ⓢ Cork Hill • Map E4 • Open 10am–5:15pm Mon–Sat • Adm

Grafton Street

Considered to be the premier shopping street on the south side of the Liffey, Grafton Street is also a pedestrianized venue for street musicians, performers and flower-sellers. There is the usual eclectic mix of high-street shops, and ugly neon signs clash with the more classical features of

City Hall

Grafton Street

such shop fronts as Marks & Spencer. The street runs south from College Green, marked by the statue of Molly Malone (irreverently known as "the tart with the cart"), opening out onto St Stephen's Green at the southern end. Brown Thomas (see p57) is one of the street's famous high-class department stores and there are numerous pubs in the surrounding side streets offering welcome refreshments for the tired shopper. Ⓢ Map E5

Powerscourt Townhouse
Built in the 18th century for Viscount Powerscourt, this fine building was converted into a shopping precinct in 1981. The main, grand entrance opens into a fine hall and staircase. The Georgian Room on the first floor, now turned into a shop similar to the other reception rooms, has exquisite plasterwork created by Michael Stapleton. There is a variety of stores here, including jewellery designers, trendy boutiques, craft outlets, coffee specialists and greengrocers. When you have exhausted your shopping cravings, there are plenty of places to eat and drink.
Ⓢ S William St • Map E4

A Day Exploring the Southside

Morning

Breakfast in style at **The Westbury Hotel** (see p128) then spend the first half of the morning exploring the shops on **Grafton Street** and in **Powerscourt Townhouse** and soaking up the atmosphere of the street entertainers. Once the crowds move in, continue down to College Green and walk under the arch into **Trinity College** (see pp8–9) to relax in the grounds. On leaving Trinity, head down Dame Street to **Temple Bar** (see pp18–19) and enjoy the many shops and galleries here.

For lunch, press on to Leo Burdock's, the city's oldest fish-and-chip shop (2 Werburgh St). It's take-away only so make for **Christ Church Cathedral** (see pp20–21) and sit and admire its exterior while eating. Then wander inside to view the restored crypt and treasury.

Afternoon

After lunch, retrace your steps to **Dublin Castle** (see pp14–17) for a tour of the state apartments and a visit to the Chester Beatty Library. A cup of eastern-flavoured coffee and a slice of exotic cake in the café here will set you up for your final stretch of the day. Walk down Dame and Nassau streets to Clare Street and the Millennium Wing of the **National Gallery** (see pp12–13).

Finally, to unwind (albeit on rather a hard chair), check out an evening concert at **St Patrick's Cathedral** (see pp22–3).

Left & Centre **Government Buildings** Right **Merrion Square**

TOP10 Best of the Rest

1 Dublinia
Entered via Christ Church Cathedral *(see pp20–21)*, this exhibition uses audiovisuals to recreate medieval Dublin. ⊗ *St Michael's Hill • Map C4 • Open 10am–6:30pm daily • Adm*

2 Ha'Penny Bridge
Built in 1816 to link the north and south sides of the Liffey, a halfpenny toll was once charged to cross it. ⊗ *Map E3*

3 Government Buildings
Originally the Royal College of Science, these buildings were taken over by the government after independence. ⊗ *Upper Merrion St • Map G5 • Open Sat tours only • Adm*

4 Mansion House
This graceful building has been official residence of the Lord Mayor since 1715, when the city bought it from aristocrat Joshua Dawson. ⊗ *Dawson St • Map F5 • Closed to the public*

5 Bank of Ireland
Dublin's first Palladian-style building, built for the Irish Parliament in 1739, is beautifully floodlit at night. ⊗ *College Green • Map F4 • Tours of House of Lords 10:30am, 11:30am & 1:45pm Tue*

6 Natural History Museum
Stuffed animals and skeletons illustrate the natural world through the ages. ⊗ *Merrion St • Map G5 • Open 10am–5pm Tue–Sat, 2–5pm Sun • Free • Dis. access ground floor*

7 Leinster House
This 18th-century home to the parliamentary chambers has two façades designed to reflect their views, the town house façade facing Kildare Street and the country house side looking on to Merrion Square. ⊗ *Kildare St • Map G5 • Open by appt only*

8 Merrion Square
One of the largest and grandest of Dublin's Georgian squares, lined with stately buildings. Oscar Wilde *(see p34)* is one of many illustrious past residents of the square. ⊗ *Map G5*

9 Iveagh Gardens
These little-known gardens are a lovely place to relax beside the rose bushes. ⊗ *Map E6*

10 The Little Museum of Dublin
This quirky museum features over 5,000 artifacts donated by the public, which tell the story of Dublin in the 20th century. ⊗ *15 St Stephen's Green, Dublin 2 • Map F5 • 01-661 1000 • Open 9:30am–5pm daily (until 8pm Thu) • Adm*

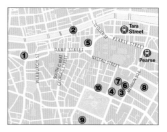

Left **Brown Thomas** Right **House of Ireland**

🔟 Southside Shops

Brown Thomas
The smartest department store in town. A couple of floors of designer labels give the fashionistas plenty of scope, and there's also a great glass and china department featuring top Irish designs. ✆ *Grafton St • Map E5*

Kilkenny Shop
The best of Irish contemporary design in fashion, art, ceramics and glass are available here at reasonable prices, so it is a great place to pick up a unique souvenir. ✆ *6–15 Nassau St • Map F4*

Hodges Figgis
Established in 1768, this is Ireland's oldest bookshop. Floors full of books covering all subjects and very good bargain offers available. Excellent children's section too. ✆ *56–8 Dawson St • Map F5*

House of Ireland
Somewhat geared towards the tourist but nonetheless with an interesting range of Irish-made items, predominantly clothes, gifts and Waterford Crystal *(see p83)*. ✆ *37–8 Nassau St • Map F4*

Designyard Gallery
Excellent gallery shop with highly original pieces of contemporary Irish and European jewellery, sculpture and art by over 100 designers. ✆ *25 South Frederick St • Map F5*

Celtic Note
This small shop specializes in Irish music records and CDs; it is difficult to pass by without being lured in by the Celtic tunes wafting into the street. ✆ *14–15 Nassau St • Map F4*

Avoca Handweavers
An Aladdin's cave. Beautiful and contemporary homeware – blankets, throws and cushions – sit alongside gorgeous own-label fashions. Excellent food section, with a restaurant on the top floor and a deli in the basement. ✆ *11–13 Suffolk St • Map E4*

James Fox
A Dublin institution, James Fox's cigarette and cigar emporium is definitely a place for connoisseurs. Specializes in Cuban and other fine cigars, and a wide range of smoking accessories. ✆ *119 Grafton St • Map F4*

Kevin & Howlin
A traditional shop selling everything tweedy for men and women with conservative tastes, including the famous Donegal tweed. Wonderful old-fashioned service too. ✆ *31 Nassau St • Map F4*

Celtic Whiskey Shop
This cosy shop offers a dazzling array of local Irish whiskeys in addition, of course, to the more famous brands. The service is as warm as a nip of the *uisce beatha* (water of life). ✆ *27–8 Dawson St • Map F5*

➤ *For tips on shopping in Dublin* **See p125**

Left **The International Bar** Centre **O'Neills** Right **McDaids**

Pubs and Bars

1 No Name Bar
Tucked away behind Kelly's hotel, above the popular L'Gueuleton restaurant (see p48), is the hugely sought-after hang-out, the "Secret" or "No Name Bar". It has a stylish crowd, a good smoking area and beautiful rooms with high ceilings. ◈ 3 Fade St • Map E5 • 01-648 0011

2 The Odeon
A smart bar with plenty of space and the large windows onto the street make the place light and airy. The feel is sophisticated but the atmosphere remains relaxed. ◈ 57 Harcourt St • 01-478 2088 • Map E6

3 The International Bar
Popular with writers and musicians. The evenings of live music and comedy are exceptionally good (see p44) and well-attended. ◈ 23 Wicklow St • 01-677 9250 • Map E4

4 The Palace Bar
Right on the edge of the frantic Temple Bar quarter, this casual, welcoming old-fashioned pub attracts a mixed crowd of locals and tourists. Built in 1823, it's one of the oldest pubs in the area. ◈ 21 Fleet St • Map E3 • 01-671 7388

5 McDaids
This pub offers literary tradition and an authentic old-style Dublin drinking experience, with stained-glass windows and old wooden interior. The writer Brendan Behan used to drink here so it's a stop-off for a popular Literary Pub Crawl. ◈ 3 Harry St • 01-679 4395 • Map E5

6 Davy Byrne's
A friendly pub immortalized by James Joyce in his book Ulysses. Seafood and traditional Irish fare accompany the drink. ◈ 21 Duke St • 01-677 5217 • Map F5

7 Oliver St John Gogarty
Extremely popular with tourists for its central location in the middle of Temple Bar and more particularly for its traditional Irish food and music. ◈ 58–9 Fleet St • Map E3

8 The Market Bar
The benches in this vast designer bar in a former sausage factory soon fill up with people. Tasty tapas and an open kitchen add to the buzz. ◈ 14a Fade St • Map E5 • 01-613 9094

9 O'Neills
The exterior of this pub is authentic and old-fashioned, while inside there are several different bar areas offering a variety of experiences and clientele. ◈ 2 Suffolk St • 01-679 3656 • Map E4

10 37 Dawson St
Expect delicious eats and tempting cocktails at this hip restaurant bar in the middle of the city. The dedicated whiskey bar serves a fantastic selection from across the world. ◈ 37 Dawson St., Dublin 2 • 01-902 2908 • Map F5

For Dublin's Top 10 Pubs See pp42–3

Price Categories

For a three-course meal for one with half a bottle of wine (or equivalent meal), taxes and extra charges.

€	under €35
€€	€35–€45
€€€	€45–€65
€€€€	€65–€90
€€€€€	over €90

Above **Gotham Café**

 Places to Eat

1 Pitt Bros
An absolute must for meat lovers, Pitt Bros is known for great, affordable food. Its signature style is slow-cooked smoked meat, with the brisket and pulled pork being the favourite. ◎ *Unit 1, Wicklow House, Georges St, Dublin • Map E4 • 01-677 8777 • €*

2 Peploe's Wine Bistro
Located in an elegant Georgian basement, this wine bar has a stylish atmosphere and offers snacks as well as a rich dinner menu. ◎ *16 St Stephen's Green • Map F5 • 01-676 3144 • Dis. access • €€€€*

3 Bewley's Café and Restaurant
Right in the centre of Grafton Street (see p54), this iconic café opened in 1927 and has been a favourite spot for shoppers ever since. ◎ *78 Grafton St • Map E5 • 01-672 7720 • €*

4 The Port House
A little corner of Spanish heaven in the heart of Dublin – this cosy candlelit restaurant serves a wide selection of tapas to the pulse of Spanish music. Tasty, affordable fare and good service. ◎ *64A South William St, Dublin 2 • Map E4 • 01-677 0298 • €*

5 One Pico
A chic fine dining restaurant. Try the roasted Wicklow venison loin or the John Dory with Morteau sausage and surf clams. ◎ *5–6 Molesworth Place, Schoolhouse Lane • Map F5 • 01-676 0300 • €€€€*

6 Gotham Café
A buzzing, New York-inspired, family friendly pizza joint. ◎ *8 South Anne St • Map F5 • 01-679 5266 • €*

7 Fallon & Byrne
This is a food-lover's haven. Parisian-style cuisine in the restaurant, a large ground-floor food hall and a basement wine bar. ◎ *11–17 Exchequer St • Map E4 • 01-472 1000 • Dis. access • €€*

8 Saba
A popular Thai and Vietnamese eatery with excellent cocktails. ◎ *26–8 Clarendon St • Map E5 • 01-679 2000 • Dis. access • €€*

9 Chez Max
A perfect little piece of Paris in the heart of Dublin. Serves classics such as beef bourguignon and *moules frites*. ◎ *1 Palace St • Map D4 • 01-633 7215 • €€*

10 Yamamori Noodles
Excellent Japanese cuisine. Soups, noodles and sushi in generous proportions. ◎ *71–2 S Great George's St • Map E4 • 01-475 5001 • €€*

 Note: *Unless otherwise stated, all restaurants accept credit cards and serve vegetarian meals.*

Left **Mural, Abbey Theatre** Right **Custom House**

North of the Liffey

WHEN DUBLIN WAS DEVELOPED IN THE 18TH CENTURY, *plans for the north side of the River Liffey included a range of elegant terraces and squares designed to attract the city's élite. A downturn in the economy left the grand plan incomplete, although O'Connell Street and Parnell and Mountjoy Squares remain evidence of what might have been. The area boasts some of the city's most beautiful buildings, such as the Custom House and the Four Courts; three theatres, the Abbey, Peacock and the Gate, produce drama of worldwide acclaim; and the city's great literary tradition is celebrated in the Dublin Writers' Museum and James Joyce Cultural Centre. Although not as self-consciously stylish as the Southside, the area north of the Liffey has a unique character and charm all of its own.*

🔟 Sights

1. Parnell Square
2. O'Connell Street
3. Custom House
4. Hugh Lane Gallery
5. James Joyce Cultural Centre
6. Dublin Writers' Museum
7. Abbey & Peacock Theatres
8. General Post Office
9. Old Jameson Distillery
10. Gate Theatre

Daniel O'Connell monument

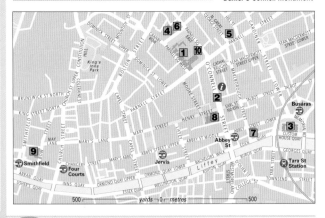

Discover more at **www.traveldk.com**

Parnell Square
The credit for this lovely Georgian square goes to Bartholomew Mosse, who founded the Rotunda Hospital here *(see p66)*. It was considered one of Dublin's smartest addresses in the 1760s, then its fortunes declined, but it remains home to some fine literary museums and art galleries. ☉ *Map E1*

O'Connell Street
One of the widest streets in Europe, O'Connell Street was designed by Luke Gardiner in the 1740s and was once lined with Classical buildings. Sadly, many of these were destroyed during the Easter Rising *(see p31)*, but one of its remaining charms is its statues, the most imposing being that of Daniel O'Connell. The Monument of Light (known as the Spire) is a latter-day iconic hallmark. ☉ *Map E2*

Custom House
This magnificent building dominates the Northside riverbank. Designed by James Gandon, the 114-m (375-ft) long façade is flanked by pavilioned arcades adorned with the Irish coats of arms. The 14 heads decorating the building represent

Custom House

Ireland's rivers. The building was burned to a shell in 1921 during the War of Independence. It was rebuilt in the late 1920s and is now used as government offices. ☉ *Custom House Quay • 01-888 2000 • Map G2 • Closed to the public*

Hugh Lane Gallery
Art-lover Hugh Lane spent his life collecting important art, and today the permanent collection includes exceptional 20th-century work by Irish and European artists, including Manet and Renoir. An addition is the Dublin-born painter Francis Bacon's London studio. ☉ *Charlemont House, Parnell Sq North • 01-222 5550 • Map E1 • Open 10am–6pm Tue–Thu, 10am–5pm Fri–Sat, 11am–5pm Sun • Free • www.hughlane.ie*

O'Connell Street

Nelson's Pillar

In the 1880s a controversial 40-m (121-ft) column topped with a 4-m (13-ft) statue of Nelson was erected in O'Connell Street. Several attempts were made over the years to destroy this symbol of British imperialism until, in 1966, a bomb damaged it so badly that it had to be dismantled.

5 James Joyce Cultural Centre

James Joyce *(see p34)* spent much of his early life living to the north of the Liffey so it is a fitting area to house a museum dedicated to the Irish writer. The house, built in 1784, was leased at the turn of the 20th century by Denis J Maginni, who makes several appearances in Joyce's epic work *Ulysses*. A copy of Joyce's death mask by sculptor Paul Speck is on view. ◈ *35 N Great George's St • 01-878 8547 • Map F1 • Open 10am–5pm Mon–Sat, noon–5pm Sun • Adm • www.jamesjoyce.ie*

6 Dublin Writers' Museum

Rare and first editions of critical works sit alongside a collection of portraits in this original little museum. The Georgian proportions of the house are seen at their best on the upper floors, with a grand Gallery of Writers. Downstairs, a taped commentary takes you through Irish literary history, accompanied by photographs and correspondence. ◈ *18 Parnell Sq North • 01-872 2077 • Map E1 • Open 10am–5pm Mon–Sat, 11am–5pm Sun • Adm • www.writersmuseum.com*

7 Abbey and Peacock Theatres

The Irish National Theatre was founded at the Abbey Theatre *(see p40)* by the Gaelic Revival Movement led by Lady Augusta Gregory and WB Yeats *(see p34)* and first opened its doors in 1904. From the outset it had a radical reputation, putting on revolutionary plays such as Sean O'Casey's *The Plough and the Stars*. The theatre then went into decline, before being gutted by fire in 1951. It reopened in 1966 as the Abbey and Peacock Theatres. The work performed at the Peacock is more experimental, while the Abbey stages conventional productions and new works. ◈ *26 Lower Abbey St • 01-878 7222 • Map F3 • www.abbeytheatre.ie*

8 General Post Office

Designed in 1814 in Neo-Classical style by Francis Johnston, the GPO is one of the city's most imposing buildings. It was the centre of the failed Easter Rising in 1916 and the scars of gunfire can still be seen on the Ionic portico. The history of this event can be seen in a sequence of paintings in the foyer by Irish artist Norman Teeling. ◈ *O'Connell St • Map E2 • Open 8am–8pm Mon–Sat • Dis. access • Free*

Dublin Writers' Museum

Chapter One Restaurant's theatre menu allows you to have a first and main course pre-performance and then return for dessert.

Old Jameson Distillery

Old Jameson Distillery

The Old Jameson Distillery now exists purely as a museum, but whiskey was first made here in the 1780s and is as much a part of the Irish culture as Guinness *(see pp24–5)*. The tour goes through the entire process of production, from grain delivery to bottling. At the end of the tour there is a whiskey tasting. The former distillery chimney is now a 67-m (220-ft) high observation platform with city views. ◈ *Bow St • 01-807 2355 • Map B3 • Open 9am–6pm Mon–Sat, 10am–6pm Sun • Adm*

Gate Theatre

Originally known as The Assembly Rooms when completed in 1786, the building, designed by the German architect Richard Cassels, was converted into the Gate Theatre by the actors Hilton Edwards and Mícheál MacLiammóir in 1928. It soon established a reputation for high-class European productions, rivalling the Abbey, which concentrated on Irish plays. The Gate has maintained its standing as a venue for new plays but also puts on excellent productions of international and Irish classics. ◈ *Cavendish Row, Parnell Sq East • 01-874 4045 • Map E1 • Dis. access*

A Day's Stroll Around the Northside

Morning

For an unusual late breakfast head for the **Cobalt Café** on North Great George's Street. Next, aim for **O'Connell Street** *(see p61)* and the **GPO**, where you can post your cards and view the historic bullet marks, and up to the **Gate Theatre** to book tickets for the evening's performance.

Be at the **Hugh Lane Gallery** *(see p61)* by 10am to have time to view the collection, then walk down to the **Dublin Writers' Museum**. Have lunch in the café before enjoying the literary artifacts. As you leave the museum, go downstairs to **Chapter One Restaurant** *(see p67)* and book a table for dinner.

Afternoon

After lunch, walk around the corner to the **James Joyce Cultural Centre**, then retrace your steps to the west side of **Parnell Square** *(see p61)* and the **Rotunda Hospital** *(see p66)* to have a look at the Baroque chapel.

For a bit of retail therapy, head for **Henry Street** *(see p46)*, one of the city's main shopping areas. Continue down St Mary's Lane and up Bow Street to the **Old Jameson Distillery** for a tour and tot of whiskey.

Walk along the river past the floodlit **Custom House** *(see p61)* to enjoy a civilized pre-theatre drink at **The Gresham** hotel *(see p129)*.

Following pages: Ha'Penny Bridge

Left **Four Courts** Right **King's Inns**

Best of the Rest

Garden of Remembrance
Opened by Eamon de Valera in 1966 on the 50th anniversary of the Easter Rising *(see p31)*, this peaceful park commemorates all those who died in the fight for Irish Freedom. ✆ *Parnell Sq • 01-821 3021 • Map E1 • Open dawn–dusk • Free*

Rotunda Hospital
Designed by Richard Cassels, this was the first purpose-built maternity hospital in Europe when it opened in 1745. Inside is a beautiful Baroque chapel. ✆ *Parnell Sq • Map E1*

St Mary's Pro Cathedral
Catholic Dublin has not had its own cathedral since the Reformation, but St Mary's has been playing the part since 1825. It is home to the Palestrina choir, who sing the Sunday morning service. ✆ *83 Marlborough St • 01-874 5441 • Map F2 • Open 9.30am–5pm Mon–Fri, 9.30am–2.30pm Sat • Free*

Four Courts
This James Gandon master-piece is a majestic blend of Corinthian columns, copper lantern dome, arcades and arches. ✆ *Inns Quay • 01-888 6459 • Map C3 • Open 10am–5pm when court is sitting • Free*

National Museum – Decorative Arts & History
Exhibits include Soldiers and Chiefs (military history), The Way We Wore (fashion) and Irish silver. ✆ *Collins Barracks, Benburb St • Map A3 • Open 10am–5pm Tue–Sat, 2–5pm Sun*

King's Inns
Designed by James Gandon in the 1790s as a training school for barristers. ✆ *Henrietta St, Constitution Hill • 01-874 4840 • Map C1 • Grounds only, open to the public*

Smithfield
This redeveloped cobbled area, home to horse fairs on the first Sunday of the month, is also used for concerts. ✆ *Map B3*

St Mary's Abbey
Founded in 1139. All that remains of the abbey is the vaulted chapterhouse. ✆ *Meetinghouse Lane • Map D3 • Closed until further notice • Free tours*

St Michan's Church
The attraction at this 11th-century church is the macabre mummified bodies. ✆ *Church St • 01-872 4154 • Map C3 • Open 10am–12:45pm & 2–4:45pm Mon–Fri, 10am–12:45pm Sat • Dis. access • Adm*

GAA Museum
The Gaelic Athletic Association offers an insight into Irish sports. ✆ *Croke Park • Drumcondra Station • 01-819 2323 • Open 9:30am–5pm Mon–Sat, noon–5pm Sun • Adm*

Price Categories

For a three-course meal for one with half a bottle of wine (or equivalent meal), taxes and extra charges.

€	under €35
€€	€35–€45
€€€	€45–€65
€€€€	€65–€90
€€€€€	over €90

Left **Chapter One** Right **The Winding Stair**

🔟 Places to Eat

1 Ely Bar & Brasserie
A lively waterside eatery that offers a wide range of wines and delicious food made from local organic ingredients. Outdoor seating is available in summer. ◈ *IFSC • Map H2 • 01-672 0010 • €€*

2 Chapter One
Warm colours, comfortable seating and courteous service set the tone. Excellent "pre-theatre" dinner menu *(see p63)* and Irish and French cuisine. ◈ *18–19 Parnell Sq • Map E1 • 01-873 2266 • €€€*

3 The Cobalt Café
A bright and airy café that serves home-made soups, sandwiches and cakes, alongside an array of vegetarian stews and tarts. The walls are adorned with paintings by up-and-coming Irish artists, making Cobalt a popular haunt for art lovers. ◈ *16 North Great Georges St • Map E1 • 01-873 0313 • €*

4 101 Talbot
Just around the corner from the Abbey Theatre. Curries and traditional classics are complemented by an extensive vegetarian menu. ◈ *101–2 Talbot St • Map F2 • 01-874 5011 • €€*

5 Panem
This tiny eatery is a great place to take gorgeous filled foccacias and croissants out on to the boardwalk in the summer, or instead enjoy the chic interiors. ◈ *21 Lower Ormond Quay • Map E3 • 01-872 8510 • Open 9am–5pm • €*

6 Ristorante Romano
A traditional Italian restaurant with cycling memorabilia on the walls and classics on the menu. Hearty portions, friendly service and a cosy atmosphere. ◈ *12 Capel St • Map D3 • 01-872 6868 • Dis. access • €*

7 Govinda's
Just the place for vegetarians on a budget looking for a tasty meal. ◈ *83 Middle Abbey St • Map F2 • Dis. access • €*

8 Epicurean Food Hall
International food emporium with everything from kebabs to Italian faro. ◈ *1 Liffey St Lower • 01 283 6077 • Map E3 • Open 9am–7pm Mon–Wed (until 8pm Thu–Sat), 11am–7pm Sun • €*

9 The Winding Stair
An attractively simple restaurant offering the best of Irish produce, try the potted beer braised kettle duck. ◈ *40 Lwr Ormond Quay • Map E3 • 01-872 7320 • €€€*

10 Harbourmaster
An old-style pub in the heart of the docklands, serving modern dishes like burgers and pasta. ◈ *Customs House Dock, IFSC • Map G3 • 01-670 1688 • Dis. access • €€*

Note: *Unless otherwise stated, all restaurants serve vegetarian meals, and all accept credit cards.*

Left **Phoenix Park** Centre **Powerscourt** Right **Kilmainham Gaol**

Greater Dublin

THE AREA AROUND DUBLIN'S CITY CENTRE IS RICH WITH ATTRACTIONS, from stunning country estates – survivors of the Georgian heyday – to ancient Celtic remains and some spectacular scenery and walks, both in man-made landscaped surroundings or wilder natural settings. As in days gone by, many of Ireland's wealthy and well known choose to live in Dublin County's peaceful villages, benefiting from their close proximity to the capital while enjoying a more traditional way of life. The ten sights selected here are less than an hour from Dublin as long as the journeys are undertaken outside the rush hours. A number of companies run day- or half-day trips to most of the sights within easy reach of Dublin.

Russborough House

🔟 Sights

1. Guinness Storehouse
2. Kilmainham Gaol & Hospital
3. Phoenix Park
4. Powerscourt Estate
5. Castletown House
6. Russborough
7. Glendalough
8. National Stud
9. Newgrange & the Boyne Valley
10. Newbridge Demesne

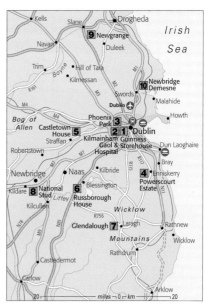

1 Guinness Storehouse

To the west of the centre, this comprehensive exhibition, set in the old brewery building, takes the visitor step-by-step through the creation of the famous beer, from the grain to the final glass of creamy topped black liquid (see pp24–5).

2 Kilmainham Gaol and Hospital

At the far west of the city, these two institutions could not be more different. The forbidding Kilmainham Gaol, with its grim history, was restored and opened as a museum in the 1960s; in contrast, the former hospital is a fine and beautiful building, restored in the 1980s and now home to the Irish Museum of Modern Art (see pp26–7).

3 Phoenix Park

There is enough to see within this vast park to keep the visitor busy for a whole day. The zoo is one of the main attractions, and Áras an Uachtaráin provides the official home to the President of Ireland (see pp28–9).

4 Powerscourt Estate

Five minutes from the pretty village of Enniskerry, Powerscourt Estate is a magnificent spot. The visitor approaches the house down a long beech-lined avenue with beautiful views across the valley. The house, designed by Richard Cassels in the 1730s,

Powerscourt

Castletown House

was gutted by fire in 1974, but a small exhibition gives the "before and after" story of its reconstruction. The main part of the house is now given over to an up-market shop (see p75) and large restaurant. The gardens are spread over a steep slope looking across to Sugar Loaf Mountain; steps lead down to a lake, where a Triton fountain hurls water high into the air.
⊛ Enniskerry, Co Wicklow • 01-204 6000 • Map N5 • Open 9:30am–5:30pm daily; (until dusk in winter) • Dis. access • Adm • www.powerscourt.com

5 Castletown House

This was the first example of Palladianism to be constructed in Ireland (1722–9) and remains the largest and most significant of its kind in the country. Architects Alessandro Galilei and Sir Edward Lovett Pearce built the house for William Conolly, the Speaker of the Irish Parliament. The fine interiors were commissioned in the second half of the 18th century by Lady Louisa Lennox, the wife of Conolly's great-nephew Tom, who took up residence here in 1758. The house remained in the family until 1965 and, after a period of ownership by the Georgian Society, is now run by the state. ⊛ Celbridge, Co Kildare • 01-628 8252 • Map N5 • Open mid-Mar–Oct: 10:15am–5pm • Dis. access • Adm

Tour company buses to areas outside Dublin depart from the Central Bus Station, Busarus, in Store Street.

69

Gatehouses, Glendalough

Russborough

Another fine Palladian mansion, claiming the longest frontage in Ireland, Russborough was designed by Richard Cassels in the mid-18th century. Standing on raised ground it faces a stretch of water backed by the Wicklow Mountains *(see pp80–81)* and is kept in immaculate condition. One of the main reasons to visit is for the outstanding Beit Art Collection, put together in the 19th century by Sir Alfred Beit (1853–1906). His nephew bought Russborough in 1952 to house the collection.
⊗ *Blessington, Co Wicklow • 045 865 239 • Map N5 • Open Mar–Sep: 10am–5pm Sat & Sun, noon–3pm Mon–Fri • Dis. access • Adm • www.russboroughhouse.ie*

Glendalough

A large part of the charm of this important monastic site is its location. The name translates as the "valley of the two lakes": the Upper Lake provides some of the most splendid scenery, with wooded slopes and a plunging waterfall, while the Lower Lake has a feeling of spirituality with the monastic ruins all around. St Kevin, a member of the Leinster royal family, founded the monastery during the 6th century and it became a renowned centre of Celtic learning. ⊗ *Co Wicklow • 040 445 325 • Map N5 • Open daily*

National Stud

Visitors can tour this state-run bloodstock farm to learn about the breeding and training of these fine racehorses. The museum charts the development of the stud since its establishment by Colonel Hall Walker in 1900. Also within the estate are the Japanese Gardens, laid out between 1906–10 by Hall Walker and two Japanese gardeners to represent the "life of man". St Fiachra's Garden was created to mark the Millennium, named after a 6th-century monk with a love of gardening. ⊗ *Kildare • 045 521 617 • Map N5 • Open 9am–5pm daily • Dis. access • Adm • www.irishnationalstud.ie*

Upper Lake, Glendalough

 Numbers allowed entry to the Newgrange site at one time are limited, so expect to queue in high season.

9 Newgrange and the Boyne Valley

Newgrange is one of the most significant passage graves in Europe but its origins are shrouded in mystery. Celtic legend tells that the Kings of Tara are buried here, but Newgrange was certainly constructed earlier. All visitors must pass through the excellent Brú na Bóinne Visitor Centre and join a tour. *Brú na Bóinne* ("Palace of the Boyne") is the Irish name for the area, considered to be the origin of Irish civilization. Anyone with an interest in archaeology will find the Boyne Valley fascinating – its Hills of Tara and Slane also feature in Celtic mythology. ⊗ *Boyne Valley • 041 988 0300 • Map M5 • Opening hours vary, but always open 9:30am–5pm daily • Adm • www.newgrange.com*

10 Newbridge Demesne

A must for architecture fans, this attractive house lies north of Dublin at the seaside village of Donabate. The house was designed for Archbishop Charles Cobbe in 1737 by George Semple – the Cobbe family still live in the upper half of the house although the council bought it from them in the 1980s. Rooms include the beautifully preserved Red Drawing Room, the huge kitchen and the Museum of Curiosities. ⊗ *Donabate • 01-843 6534 • Map M5 • House and Farm: see website for opening hours • Adm • www.newbridge houseandfarm.com*

Newbridge Demesne

A Drive Around Greater Dublin

Morning

🕐 Head out of Dublin on the N4 west road to Celbridge and **Castletown House** *(see p69)*. Take the first tour and you will get an excellent history of the house and family as well as being talked through the architectural highlights. Negotiate your way back to the Naas Road (N7) via Clane, across the Curragh towards Kildare and the **National Stud** – there's an excellent café here for a coffee. After a leisurely wander around the gardens, enjoy the fascinating and informative tour through the business of bloodstock.

After leaving here head for **Russborough House** by returning to Naas and taking the N81 Blessington road. The café-cum-restaurant at Russborough serves simple but delicious home-made fare for lunch. Then tour the house and savour the views of the **Wicklow Mountains** *(see pp80–81)*.

Afternoon

Retrace your steps to Naas and the N7 to Dublin and follow signs for **Kilmainham Gaol** *(see pp26–7)*. After a sombre visit to this former prison, cut across to **Kilmainham Hospital** for the Irish Museum of Modern Art. If further refreshment is required, there's a good café in the basement. Standing in the formal gardens here you get a great view across to **Phoenix Park** *(see pp28–9)* which you could visit on your way back into the centre, energy levels permitting.

Following pages: **Powerscourt Estate**

Left **Malahide Castle** Centre **Howth** Right **Avondale House**

🔟 Best of the Rest

1 Glasnevin Botanic Gardens and Cemetery

This garden features rare species of plants. Nearby, Ireland's Necropolis is the resting place for famous writers and revolutionaries ⊙ *Glasnevin Hill • Map N6 • Open Mar–Oct: 9am–6pm daily; Nov–Feb: 9am–4:30pm Mon–Fri, 10am–4:30pm Sat & Sun • Dis. access • Free • www.botanicgardens.ie*

2 Malahide Castle

With its five ghosts and rounded towers, this castle has a fairy-tale quality. ⊙ *Malahide • 01-816 9538 • Map N6 • Open daily • Adm*

3 Howth

This busy fishing port offers great walks around the headland. Look out for seals when the boats come in. ⊙ *Map N6*

4 Sandycove Martello Tower

The first chapter of *Ulysses (see p34)* was set here and a museum contains Joyce memorabilia. ⊙ *Sandycove • 01-280 9265 • Map N6 • Open Apr–Aug: call for details • Adm*

5 Killruddery House

Home to the Earls of Meath since 1618, the formal gardens are its main feature. ⊙ *Bray • 01-286 3405 • Map N6 • Visiting times vary, check website • Adm • www.killruddery.com*

6 Mount Usher Gardens

A lure for all garden-lovers for its rare shrubs, flowers and trees. ⊙ *Ashford • 0404 40205 • Map N6 • Open Mar–Oct: 10am–5:20pm daily • Adm*

7 Avondale House

Charles Stewart Parnell *(see p31)* was born in Avondale House, which is now a museum dedicated to his memory. ⊙ *Rathdrum, Co Wicklow • 0404 46111 • Map N6 • Open Jun–Aug: 11am–5pm daily, Sep–Oct: 11am–4pm Tue–Sun • Adm*

8 Killiney Hill Park

It is worth the climb for the spectacular views over Dublin Bay. ⊙ *Co Dublin • Map U3*

9 The Bog of Allen Nature Centre

This exhibition on Irish bogs is in the heart of the Bog of Allen *(see p99)*. ⊙ *Rathangan • Map M5 • Open 9am–4pm Mon–Fri • Adm*

10 Marino Casino

Built in the 1750s for the Earl of Charlemont, the casino was to serve as a summerhouse. It is considered among the finest 18th-century Neo-Classical buildings in Europe. ⊙ *Off Malahide Rd, Marino • 01-833 1618 • Map N6 • Open mid-Mar–Oct: 10am–5pm daily • Adm*

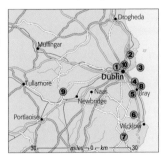

Left **Dalkey** Right **Avoca Handweavers**

🔟 Greater Dublin Shopping Areas

Powerscourt
Spread over two floors of the main house *(see p69)* are numerous different outlets. Avoca is the main retailer but there are plenty of others, including Waterford Crystal and Global Village interiors. The garden centre is also excellent. 🛍 *Powerscourt House, Enniskerry • Map N6*

Fishers of Newtownmountkennedy
An unlikely place to find tucked away here, selling up-market women's fashions and traditional men's country clothes. 🛍 *The Old Schoolhouse, Newtownmountkennedy • 01-281 9404 • Map N6 • www. fishers.ie*

Malahide
An extremely attractive village with its streets arranged in a cross-grid pattern. There are a variety of shops to visit including an excellent wine shop, designer boutiques and a well-stocked hardware store. 🛍 *Map N6*

Dalkey
Another pretty seaside village, and the home of many international stars. There are a couple of excellent galleries and designer boutiques selling pure linen clothes and original silk knitwear. 🛍 *Map N6*

Avoca Handweavers
The flagship Avoca store stocks a wide range of their own-label clothes, gifts and foods. The self-serve restaurant sells huge helpings of Mediterranean food. 🛍 *Kilmacanogue, Co Wicklow • 01-274 6900 • Map N6 • www. avoca.ie*

Mount Usher Gardens
This arcade of shops includes French label casual wear, equestrian clothes and equipment, an ice-cream parlour, art gallery and a pottery *(see p74)*.

Kildare Village
This outlet shopping centre sells designer brands at discounted prices. There are plenty of nice cafés if you need a break from the shops and an express bus runs from Dublin Airport. 🛍 *Nurney Road, Kildare town • 045 520 501 • Map N5*

Dundrum Town Centre
Said to be the largest shopping centre in Ireland, the massive Dundrum Centre has over 160 shops, including Harvey Nichols and House of Fraser as well as a cinema, restaurants and a theatre. 🛍 *Dundrum • Map T2*

Glasthule & Sandycove
These two pretty villages sit side-by-side along the seashore and are packed with boutiques and food sellers. Caviston's Food Emporium on Glasthule Road is a real delight. 🛍 *Map N6*

Wrights of Howth
Right on the pier, Wrights has a great selection of fresh fish – try the wild smoked salmon or gravadlax. 🛍 *14 West Pier, Howth • 01-816 7347 • Map N6*

Around Town – Greater Dublin

75

Left **Johnnie Fox** Right **The Gravity Bar**

Pubs and Bars

Johnnie Fox's
A well-known and respected pub, 5 km (3 miles) from Enniskerry. The 18th-century inn is full of old beams and roaring open fires, and has a seemingly endless series of connected rooms. Daniel O'Connell (see p31) was one of the pub's regulars and historic flyers decorate the walls. ✆ Glencullen • 01-295 5647 • Map N6 • www.jfp.ie

The Gravity Bar
This is the highest point of the Guinness Storehouse and has stupendous views across the city. Enjoy your free pint – if you've been to the exhibition – and try to spot the various city landmarks from the panoramic windows (see pp24–5).

The Roundwood Inn
Originally a 17th-century inn, this relaxing place with wooden benches and floors is usually full of ramblers. The bar food is very good. ✆ Roundwood, Co Wicklow • 01-281 8107 • Map N6

Lynhams Laragh Inn
A wonderful, welcoming pub with hearty fires and a jolly crowd of locals, just east of Glendalough. ✆ Laragh, Co Wicklow • 0404 45345 • Map N6 • www.lynhamsoflaragh.ie

The Purty Kitchen
Top-notch seafood within a stone's throw of the seafront. ✆ 3–5 Old Dunleary Rd, Monkstown • 01-284 3576 • Map U2 • www.purtykitchen.com

The Silken Thomas
This is both pub and restaurant and produces excellent and reasonably priced bar food. It is named after the fancy attire worn by Fitzgerald, famous for his rebellion against King Henry VIII in the mid-16th century (see p14). ✆ Kildare • 045 522 232 • Map N5

James Griffin Pub
This award-winning traditional pub in the pretty town of Trim is a real institution. The warm and lively atmosphere makes this an ideal place to grab a pint of Guinness after a visit to the beautiful Trim Castle. There is regular live Irish music. ✆ High St, Trim, Co. Meath • 046 943 1295 • Map M5

The Queens Bar and Restaurant
A mid-18th-century public house in south Dublin's Dalkey village with open fires and whole-some pub grub. ✆ Castle St, Dalkey, Co Dublin • 01-285 4569 • Map U3

The Merry Ploughboy Pub
If you're looking for traditional music, song and Irish dancing head to Rathfarnham, near the Dublin mountains, for a night of Irish charm. ✆ Rockbrook, Edmondstown Rd, Rathfarnham • 01-493 1495 • Map T2

Abbey Tavern
There's a great atmosphere in this 16th-century inn, making the most of its antique features and traditional Irish evenings. ✆ 28 Abbey St, Howth • 01-839 0307 • Map N6

Above **King Sitric**

Price Categories

For a three-course	€	under €35
meal for one with half	€€	€35–€45
a bottle of wine (or	€€€	€45–€65
equivalent meal), taxes	€€€€	€65–€90
and extra charges.	€€€€€	over €90

🔟 Places to Eat

1 King Sitric
Right at the end of Howth's harbourfront is this respected restaurant. The freshest seafood is on offer in comfortable surroundings. Good views from the first floor. Reservations essential. 🌐 *East Pier, Howth • Map N6 • 01-832 5235 • Dis. access • €€€*

2 Bon Appetit
Chef Oliver Dunne earned a Michelin star within one year of opening. He developed his prodigious skills working for Gary Rhodes and Gordon Ramsey. 🌐 *9 James Terrace, Malahide • Map N6 • 01-845 0314 • Dis. access • €€€€*

3 Hungry Monk
A slightly quirky but high-quality restaurant, specializing in game and fish. A wine bar on the ground floor is an excellent addition to the village. 🌐 *Church Rd, Greystones • Map N6 • 01-287 5759 • €€*

4 The Osborne Brasserie
Named after the artist, Walter Osborne, this restaurant offers spectacular views of Dublin Bay. The food is hearty with an emphasis on seafood. 🌐 *Portmarnock Hotel and Golf Links, Strand Rd • Map N6 • 01-846 0611 • €€*

5 Poppies
Cheerful cottage-style restaurant that resembles an English tearoom. Generous portions of reliable home cooking. 🌐 *The Square, Enniskerry • Map N6 • 01-282 8869 • €*

6 Hartley's
A very special restaurant in what used to be the Customs Hall. Lots of space and light with high ceilings and attractive decor. The seafood menu is delicious. 🌐 *1 Harbour Rd, Dun Laoghaire • Map N6 • 01-280 6767 • Dis. access • €€*

7 Mao
The space here is big and airy, overlooking Dun Laoghaire harbour. The food is Asian style – quick and delicious. 🌐 *The Pavilion, Dun Laoghaire • Map N6 • 01-214 8090 • Dis. access • €*

8 Cavistons
This small, smart restaurant has a reputation for producing mouth-watering fish dishes. It is open for lunch with three sittings, and also for dinner on Friday and Saturday. 🌐 *59 Glasthule Rd, Sandycove • Map N6 • 01-280 9245 • €€*

9 Grangecon Café
Simple and tasty food. Everything is home-made and the locally sourced ingredients are all organic. Delicious take-away breads and cakes. Open for lunch only. 🌐 *Lake Rd, Blessington, Co. Wicklow • Map S3 • 045 857 892 • €*

10 Aqua Restaurant
A picturesque location on a pier in the fishing village of Howth. Excellent continental cuisine including, of course, seafood. 🌐 *1 West Pier, Howth, Co. Dublin • Map U2 • 01-832 0690 • €€€*

Note: *Unless otherwise stated, all restaurants accept credit cards and serve vegetarian meals*

77

AROUND IRELAND

Wicklow Mountains
80–81

Around Waterford
82–85

The Ring of Kerry
and Dingle Peninsula
86–89

Around Cork
90–93

Tipperary, Limerick
and Clare
94–97

Clonmacnoise and the
Midlands
98–99

Around Galway
100–103

Connemara
and Mayo
104–107

Yeats Country
and the Northwest
108–113

Northern Ireland
114–117

DUBLIN'S TOP 10

Left **Sally Gap** Right **Wicklow Gap**

🔟 Wicklow Mountains

1 Sally Gap
This bleak and remote crossroads on the mountain road between Dublin and Glendalough stands at one of the highest mountain passes in Ireland. With its extensive areas of watery bog, the country is so inaccessible around here that it was a favourite hideout for Irish warriors and nationalist rebels during the centuries of conflicts between the English and Irish forces. ⊗ Map N5

2 Wicklow Gap
This high point on the little R756 road through the Wicklow Mountains is also on the mountain route to Glendalough from Dublin. Turn here to climb up to the 2,670-ft (816-m) Tonelagee viewpoint, with its breathtaking panoramic view. There are few places that better capture the lonely beauty of this mountain range. ⊗ Map N5

Rural cottage, Wicklow Mountains

3 Wicklow Way
For those who really want to see the mountains at close hand, there's nothing better than walking. Numerous easy marked local paths run through pretty hill country, while the Wicklow Way is for serious hikers. This 79-mile (127-km) marked path makes its way through the heart of the region, all the way from Dublin to Clonegal, in County Carlow. ⊗ Map N5

4 Blessington and The Lakes
The delightful Georgian village of Blessington is where the beautifully preserved Palladian mansion Russborough House, and its famous Beit Art Collection, is to be found *(see p70)*. From here, yet again, there are good views of the mountains while, just south of the village, the River Liffey has been dammed to form a picturesque lake reservoir, popular with Dubliners for picnic outings and watersports. ⊗ Map N5

5 Wicklow Town
Wicklow's modest county town has a low-key charm, with its harbour and unpretentious pubs. The one unmissable sight is Wicklow Gaol. A shocking tale is told at this notorious historic jailhouse (closed in 1924), where hundreds of Irish rebels were detained, often tortured and, in many cases, hanged. Evocative exhibitions fill in the background, including a section on the

deportation of the inmates to the colonies, such as Australia. ✆ 0404 61599 Map N6 • Wicklow Gaol: Open mid-Apr–Sep: 10am–6pm daily; Adm

Djouce Woods
Close to Dublin, this steeply hilly woodland is part of the Powerscourt Estate (see p69). With the beautiful Powerscourt Waterfall at its centre, it is a popular area for an outing from the city, especially for walks, picnics, jogging and orienteering. Deer and red squirrel can be seen among the oak, Sitka spruce, Douglas fir, beech and chestnut trees. ✆ Map N5

Avondale Forest Park
The beautiful Avondale Forest Park is filled with marked walks and nature trails, some of them along the bucolic setting of the River Avonmore banks. There is also an 18th-century arboretum within the park, with an impressive range of plant species. ✆ Rathdrum • Map N5 • Open Easter–31 Oct • Adm

Vale of Avoca
"There is not in the wide world a valley so sweet," wrote 19th-century poet Thomas Moore in his work The Meeting of the Waters. It is perhaps not as idyllic now as it was then, but the meeting of rust-coloured rivers among wooded hills is still enticing. Avoca Handweavers, at the nearby village (see p75), produce wonderful authentic tweeds in Ireland's oldest handweaving mill. ✆ Map N5

Devil's Glen
Although close to Wicklow Town, this romantic wooded glen, with its waterfall and chirruping birds, is a haven of peace and tranquillity. It is part of the pretty valley of the Vartry. Perfect for walking or riding, it makes a quiet escape within an hour's drive of Dublin. There are many pleasant self-catering apartments and cottages to rent, as well as stables, and other holiday facilities. ✆ Map N5

Clara Lara Fun Park
A top recreation site for families, the fun park is in the Vale of Clara, and near the village of Laragh – hence the name. Its rides are mostly based around water, but there are Go Karts, too, and the highest slide in Ireland, as well as tree-houses, climbing frames and picnic areas. ✆ Map N5 • Open weekends May; Jun–Aug: daily

View of the Wicklow Mountains

Left **Hook Peninsula** Right **Stone carving, Jerpoint Abbey**

Around Waterford

GREEN AND HILLY COUNTY WATERFORD *is exposed to the Atlantic to the south, the beautiful Blackwater and Suir rivers penetrate far inland, while Waterford City stands by an excellent natural harbour. All these factors made this corner of the southeast almost too welcoming to outsiders – Waterford City (Vadrafjord in Norse), founded in AD 853, is thought to be the oldest surviving Viking town in Europe. Later, Normans also chose this spot for their first Irish settlement – in few other places can Celtic, Norse and Norman relics be found so close to one another. In modern times, Waterford has been staunchly patriotic and proud of its heritage – it even has a small Gaeltacht (Irish-speaking district) around the village of Rinn.*

🔟 Sights

1. House of Waterford Crystal
2. Waterford Museum of Treasures
3. Waterford City Centre
4. Ardmore
5. Jerpoint Abbey
6. Hook Peninsula
7. Passage East
8. Reginald's Tower
9. Dunmore East
10. John F Kennedy Park and Arboretum

Reginald's Tower

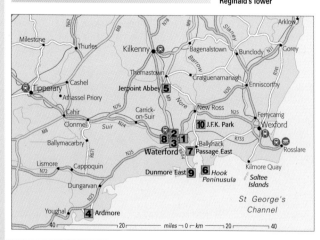

deportation of the inmates to the colonies, such as Australia.
✆ *0404 61599 Map N6 • Wicklow Gaol: Open mid-Apr–Sep: 10am–6pm daily; Adm*

Djouce Woods
Close to Dublin, this steeply hilly woodland is part of the Powerscourt Estate *(see p69)*. With the beautiful Powerscourt Waterfall at its centre, it is a popular area for an outing from the city, especially for walks, picnics, jogging and orienteering. Deer and red squirrel can be seen among the oak, Sitka spruce, Douglas fir, beech and chestnut trees. ✆ *Map N5*

Avondale Forest Park
The beautiful Avondale Forest Park is filled with marked walks and nature trails, some of them along the bucolic setting of the River Avonmore banks. There is also an 18th-century arboretum within the park, with an impressive range of plant species. ✆ *Rathdrum • Map N5 • Open Easter–31 Oct • Adm*

Vale of Avoca
"There is not in the wide world a valley so sweet," wrote 19th-century poet Thomas Moore in his work *The Meeting of the Waters*. It is perhaps not as idyllic now as it was then, but the meeting of rust-coloured rivers among wooded hills is still enticing. Avoca Handweavers, at the nearby village *(see p75)*, produce wonderful authentic tweeds in Ireland's oldest handweaving mill. ✆ *Map N5*

Devil's Glen
Although close to Wicklow Town, this romantic wooded glen, with its waterfall and chirruping birds, is a haven of peace and tranquillity. It is part of the pretty valley of the Vartry. Perfect for walking or riding, it makes a quiet escape within an hour's drive of Dublin. There are many pleasant self-catering apartments and cottages to rent, as well as stables, and other holiday facilities. ✆ *Map N5*

Clara Lara Fun Park
A top recreation site for families, the fun park is in the Vale of Clara, and near the village of Laragh – hence the name. Its rides are mostly based around water, but there are Go Karts, too, and the highest slide in Ireland, as well as tree-houses, climbing frames and picnic areas. ✆ *Map N5 • Open weekends May; Jun–Aug: daily*

View of the Wicklow Mountains

Left **Hook Peninsula** Right **Stone carving, Jerpoint Abbey**

Around Waterford

GREEN AND HILLY COUNTY WATERFORD *is exposed to the Atlantic to the south, the beautiful Blackwater and Suir rivers penetrate far inland, while Waterford City stands by an excellent natural harbour. All these factors made this corner of the southeast almost too welcoming to outsiders – Waterford City (Vadrafjord in Norse), founded in AD 853, is thought to be the oldest surviving Viking town in Europe. Later, Normans also chose this spot for their first Irish settlement – in few other places can Celtic, Norse and Norman relics be found so close to one another. In modern times, Waterford has been staunchly patriotic and proud of its heritage – it even has a small Gaeltacht (Irish-speaking district) around the village of Rinn.*

 **Sights**

1. House of Waterford Crystal
2. Waterford Museum of Treasures
3. Waterford City Centre
4. Ardmore
5. Jerpoint Abbey
6. Hook Peninsula
7. Passage East
8. Reginald's Tower
9. Dunmore East
10. John F Kennedy Park and Arboretum

Reginald's Tower

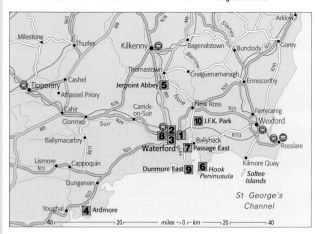

Specialist glass cutter

House of Waterford Crystal
The Waterford Crystal factory was for many years a major source of employment and local pride, but production ceased briefly at the plant in 2009. The custom-designed House of Waterford Crystal opened in 2010 in a grand old building which used to house the electricity board. About 53,000 pieces are created here annually by specialist glassblowers and cutters. Tours are available, along with a store. *The Mall, Waterford City • 051 317000 • Map Q5 • Open Mar–Oct: 9am–4:15pm daily; Nov–Feb: 9:30am–3:15pm Mon–Fri • Dis. access • Adm for tour*

Waterford Museum of Treasures
These three museums, located around Waterford city, document over 1,000 years of history. Reginald's Tower houses the Treasures of Viking Waterford, a collection of artifacts that tell the story of the city's Viking heritage. An exhibition on medieval Waterford is displayed in Choristor's Hall and the Georgian era is represented in the former Bishop's Palace, home to the oldest piece of Waterford crystal in the world – a decanter from the 1780s. *Waterford • 051 304500 • Map P5 • Open daily • Dis. access • Adm*

Waterford City Centre
Surviving sections of Waterford's city walls show clearly the limits of the original Viking settlement, also bordered on one side by the River Suir. Today that waterfront, with its lively and attractive quays, is the focal point of the town. The 18th-century City Hall houses important local memorabilia, and hosts the Waterford Show, an entertainment about the town's history. *Map P5*

Ardmore
Modern Ardmore is a popular little beach resort, but the hill behind is the site of St Declan's 5th-century monastery, probably the oldest in Ireland. Its many evocative remains (mostly dating from the 12th century) include St Declan's Cathedral, a fine example of a high cross, and an impressive, 30-m (100-ft) round tower. *Map Q4*

Jerpoint Abbey
One of Ireland's best examples of a Cistercian monastery, the restored chapterhouse and part of the cloisters of 12th-century Jerpoint stand grandly among its ruins in a peaceful countryside setting. The Jerpoint community established itself as a centre of culture and learning, and was very prosperous until the Dissolution in 1540 when it was surrendered to the crown. Many fine pieces of stone-carving can be seen, and there is a useful Interpretative Centre. *Thomastown • 056 7724623 • Map P5 • Open Mar–Sep: 9am–5:30pm daily; Oct: 9am–5pm daily; Nov: 9:30am–4pm daily; Dec–Feb: Pre-booked tours only • Dis. access • Adm*

Hook Peninsula

Hook Peninsula

The peaceful "Ring of Hook" headland lies beside the broad Waterford Harbour, with long sandy beaches, rugged cliffs, and many relics of the past. At the northeast corner, ruined Tintern Abbey – with its beautiful grounds – was founded in 1200 and, although much altered, remains atmospheric. The peninsula's wild tip, where there has been a lighthouse since the 5th century, is beloved of bird-watchers. ◈ *Map Q5 • Tintern Abbey: Open mid-May–Sep: 10am–6pm daily; Dis. access; Adm*

Passage East

A small, enjoyable ferry runs to-and-fro across Waterford Harbour from this unassuming waterside village. Its peaceful, scenic setting and handful of painted cottages make a pleasant break while waiting for the boat. It was at this spot that the Normans arrived in Ireland in 1170 and their sturdy stone tower still stands guard over the harbour. ◈ *Map Q5*

Reginald's Tower

The circular stone fortification built 1,000 years ago by Ragnvald, son of Sygtrygg, was part of the original Viking ramparts and still dominates the quayside. Over the centuries it provided a base for other invaders, including Strongbow, Henry II, King John and Richard II, as well as doing time as a prison. Today it houses an art gallery and a museum of Waterford history. ◈ *Quay, Waterford • Map P4 • Open Easter–May: 10am–5pm daily; Jun–mid-Sep: 10am–6pm daily; mid-Sep–Easter: 10am–5pm Wed–Sun • Adm*

Dunmore East

A working fishing harbour with brightly coloured boats, and cottages set among woods, this attractive village makes a favourite outing for a drink, lunch or a waterfront stroll. Many of the cottages are available for holiday lets. Nearby sandy coves include the popular Lady's Cove beach, and there are several enjoyable marked walks and hikes. ◈ *Map Q5*

John F Kennedy Park and Arboretum

Some 4,500 international species of trees and shrubs – all carefully labelled – grow in this delightful 600-acre arboretum, created in memory of the former US president. Visit the Kennedy Homestead in New Ross and see the birthplace of his great-grandfather. ◈ *New Ross • Map P5 • Open 10am–dusk daily • Dis. access • Adm*

Waterford's Gaeltacht

The only Irish-speaking area in the southeast is in County Waterford. The village and peninsula of Rinn, on the south side of Dungarvon Harbour, is known as the *Déise* after the *Déise* tribe whose home this was. A Gaelic College here offers further education in the language.

Price Categories

For a three-course	€ under €35
meal for one with half	€€ €35–€45
a bottle of wine (or	€€€ €45–€65
equivalent meal), taxes	€€€€ €65–€90
and extra charges.	€€€€€ over €90

Above **Dunbrody Country House**

🔟 Places to Eat

1 Lady Helen Dining Room
One of the region's more sophisticated restaurants serves an imaginative menu with international influences. It has one Michelin star and three AA rosettes. ® *Mount Juliet, Thomastown • Map P5 • 056 777 3000 • Dis. access • €€€€*

2 Bianconi
This award-winning hotel restaurant serves the best of contemporary, Italian-influenced cuisine and has an excellent wine list. ® *Granville Hotel, Waterford • Map P5 • 051 305555 • Dis. access • €€*

3 Ocean Hotel
This excellent restaurant has won awards for its menu, which is strong on freshly caught local seafood. ® *Dunmore East • Map Q5 • 051 385314 • €€*

4 Rinuccini
This multi award-winning restaurant serves an appetizing blend of classic Italian dishes and the best of modern Irish cooking (with the emphasis on seafood, game, and Irish beef and lamb). ® *1 The Parade, Kilkenny • Map P4 • 056 776 1575 • €€*

5 Dunbrody Country House
Owner Kevin Dundon is regarded as one of Ireland's finest cooks, and the restaurant of this fine country house hotel is elegant, with outstanding food and an excellent wine list. ® *Arthurstown • Map P5 • 051 389600 • Dis. access • €€€*

6 La Bohème
An elegant French restaurant situated in the vaults of a historic building. The decor is bright and the contemporary menu offers modern delicacies. ® *2 George's St, Waterford • Map Q5 • 051 875645 • Dis. access • €€*

7 Greenacres Bistro
An attractive Italian restaurant with its own art gallery, Greenacres is popular for its delicious food and the exceptional wine list. ® *Selskar, Wexford • Map P5 • 053 912 2975 • €€*

8 The Lobster Pot
This cheerful pub-restaurant near the sea (prettily decorated with hanging baskets) serves fine seafood at a price that won't break your budget. ® *Carnsore Point, Carne • Map P5 • 053 913 1110 • Dis. access (partial) • €€*

9 La Dolce Vita
This Italian restaurant, owned and run by Roberto and Celine Pons, makes simple, delicious food. A gem, dedicated to the day trade. ® *6–7 Trimmers Lane, Wexford • Map P5 • 053 917 0806 • €*

10 The Tannery
Don't miss out on chef Paul Flynn's award-winning modern Irish cuisine, using local ingredients such as seafood, poultry and game. ® *10 Quay St, Dungarvan, Waterford • Map Q4 • 058 45420 • Dis. access • €€*

Note: *Unless otherwise stated, all restaurants accept credit cards and serve vegetarian meals*

Left **Lacemaking, Kenmare** Right **Caha Mountain, Beara Peninsula**

The Ring of Kerry and the Dingle Peninsula

THE SOUTHWEST OF IRELAND IS ONE OF THE MOST BEAUTIFUL *regions of the country. The Killarney National Park is an experience in itself but, if at all possible, like the Ring of Kerry, should be seen off-season – the area has become so popular that driving the Ring can turn into a nightmare of tour buses in high season. The area is largely made up of peninsulas, the stunning Dingle Peninsula to the north, Iveragh, the largest, in the middle, and the most popular, the Beara Peninsula, with two impressive mountain ranges running along its spine, offering wonderfully dramatic views. Yet, it's not all nature. Amid this landscape, both peaceful and rugged in turns, are some striking Georgian residences, numerous pretty villages, wildlife reserves and ancient religious sites. A journey to this corner of the country will have something to suit all tastes and expectations.*

Gallarus Oratory

🔟 Sights

1. Lakes of Killarney
2. Beara Peninsula
3. Dingle
4. Kenmare
5. Bantry Bay & Bantry House
6. Gallarus Oratory
7. Killarney
8. Derrynane House
9. Sneem
10. Valentia Island and the Skelligs

Lakes of Killarney
The three lakes in this region, Upper, Middle (Muckross) and Lower (Lough Leane), are linked by the Long Range channel and are all incorporated into the stunning 103-sq km (40-sq mile) Killarney National Park. Flanked by mountains, and with a varied landscape of woodland, heather and peat bogs, the area offers a range of beautiful walks and drives. ⊗ *Killarney, Co Kerry • Map Q2*

Beara Peninsula
The largest of the western peninsulas has something for everyone, with its pretty villages, beaches and mountains. The two ranges here are the Slieve Miskish and Caha Mountains. Tortuous bends wend their way to the summits, but it's worth it for the view on fine days. If you are interested in wildlife, take the cable car across to Dursey Island, with its seabird colonies. ⊗ *Co Cork and Co Kerry • Map Q1*

Dingle
A small, attractive fishing town with a fine natural harbour, Dingle is extremely popular with tourists, who appreciate its charm. Fungi the dolphin is the town's most famous resident and people come for miles to see him play. ⊗ *Co Kerry • Map Q1*

Dingle harbour

Kenmare
Designed by the Marquis of Lansdowne in 1775, this prosperous town has more of a continental atmosphere here than Irish, with its smart shops and fine restaurants. Kenmare's greatest claim to fame, however, is more traditional, as a centre of lacemaking. ⊗ *Co Kerry • Map Q2*

Bantry Bay and Bantry House
This market town and fishing port is named after its beautiful situation at the head of Bantry Bay. Bantry House, commanding an outstanding position with views across the bay, has been owned by the White family since 1739. The stunning gardens are continuously being restored and the delightful tearoom serves home-made cakes and scones. ⊗ *Bantry, Co Cork • Map Q2 • Bantry House: Open Apr–Oct: 10am–5pm Tue–Sun • Adm • www.bantryhouse.com*

Upper Lake, Killarney

The Skelligs

The history of the Skellig Islands dates back to the 6th century when St Fionán founded the monastery of Skellig Michael. All that remains now are the ruins of the church, two oratories and six beehive cells perched on a narrow platform. From 1821 to as recently as 1981, the lighthouses here were looked after by solitary lighthousekeepers. Skellig Michael was designated a World Heritage Site in 1996.

Gallarus Oratory

The best preserved early Christian site in Ireland is believed to have been built some time between the 7th and 8th centuries AD. Local legend has it that if you climbed out of the oratory window your soul would be cleansed – an impossible task, since the window is about 18 cm (7 in) long and 12 cm (5 in) wide. *Ballydavid, Co Kerry • Map Q1 • Visitor centre 066-915 5333*

Killarney

On the doorstep of the Ring of Kerry, with a wealth of excellent hotels and old-fashioned ponies and traps, it's not surprising that this attractive town becomes inundated with visitors in summer. The shops and restaurants are worth the visit, let alone the surrounding scenery. *Co Kerry • Map Q2*

Killarney

Sneem

Derrynane House

Derrynane is a lovely spot on the coast with 3 km (2 miles) of dunes and beaches. Derrynane House is 3.5 km (2 miles) from Caherdaniel and is set in 120 hectares (300 acres) of parkland. It was the family home of Catholic politician and lawyer Daniel O'Connell *(see p31)* and now contains a museum dedicated to the great leader. *Co Kerry • 066 947 5113 • Map Q1 • Adm*

Sneem

This pretty village, backed by the 684-m (2,244-ft) Knockmoyle Mountain, resembles something out of a children's picture book, with its houses all painted different colours. A popular, friendly place. *Co Kerry • Map Q2*

Valentia Island and the Skelligs

The Skellig Experience visitor centre, near the causeway linking Valentia Island to the mainland, includes exhibits on the history of the Skellig Michael monastic site and a range of information on local flora and fauna. Valentia is a popular holiday spot and is particularly good for watersports, but the only inhabitants of the Skelligs now are the birds. Cruises circle the islands but do not land. *Co Kerry • Map Q1*

Price Categories

For a three-course meal for one with half a bottle of wine (or equivalent meal), taxes and extra charges.

€ under €35
€€ €35–€45
€€€ €45–€65
€€€€ €65–€90
€€€€€ over €90

Above **Bantry House**

🔟 Places to Eat

1 Packies
The hallmark of Maura Foley's cooking is simplicity and purity of ingredients. Relaxed and informal setting. ◈ *Henry St, Kenmare • Map Q2 • 064 6641508 • Closed Sun, Nov–Easter • €€€*

2 Sheen Falls
Everything about the Sheen Fall Lodge is grand. The hotel is immaculately run, exuding sophisticated style. The La Cascade restaurant is no exception and the food is faultless. ◈ *Kenmare, Co Kerry • Map Q2 • 064 6641600 • Dis. access • €€€€*

3 QC's Seafood Bar & Restaurant
This delightful old bar is full of character. It has a nautical theme which extends to the menu – there's plenty of tasty, chargrilled seafood. ◈ *3 Main St, Cahersiveen • Map Q1 • 066 947 2244 • Dis. access • €*

4 The Half Door
This pretty cottage-kitchen restaurant is famed for its generous seafood platters, bathed in lemon butter. ◈ *John St, Dingle, Co Kerry • Map Q1 • 066 915 1600 • €€*

5 The Lime Tree
Widely acclaimed, friendly and charming, The Lime Tree serves delicious meals prepared using local produce. Try Skeaghanore free range duck with rhubarb and ginger chutney. ◈ *Shelburne St, Kenmare • Map Q2 • 064 664 1255 • €€€*

6 Nick's Restaurant
This is an extremely relaxed and jolly place very popular with the locals, with generous portions of traditional dishes. ◈ *Lower Bridge St, Killorglin, Co Kerry • Map Q2 • 066 976 1219 • Dis. access • €€*

7 Gaby's Seafood Restaurant
Run by the Maes family who have been in the business for decades, Gaby's is one of the best fish restaurants in town. ◈ *27 High St, Killarney, Co Kerry • Map Q2 • 064 6632519 • Dis. access • €€€*

8 Bantry House
This fine house *(see p87)* overlooking Bantry Bay has an excellent tearoom with informal seating. ◈ *Bantry, Co Cork • Map Q2 • 027 50047 • €*

9 Jam
This popular café also has branches in Kenmare and Cork. Expect fresh, imaginative lunches using local produce. ◈ *Old Market Lane, Killarney, Co Kerry • Map Q2 • 064 663 7716 • Dis. access • €*

10 Chart House Restaurant
This informal modern restaurant is to the east of town with windows overlooking the harbour. The food combines many flavours, with both Asian and European influences. ◈ *The Mall, Dingle, Co Kerry • Map Q1 • 066 915 2255 • Open daily in summer (Jun–Sep), call ahead for winter times • Dis. access • €€*

Note: Unless otherwise stated, all restaurants accept credit cards and serve vegetarian meals

Left **Barley Cove, Cork** Right **Cobh**

Around Cork

CORK CITY AND THE SURROUNDING AREA *are full of historic, cultural and scenic places to visit. Cork itself is a lovely city, worth one or two days' exploration, including several islands in Cork harbour formed by the two sections of the River Lee. Cobh, situated on what is known as Great Island, came into its own in the 19th century as an important naval base, due to its huge natural harbour. Close by is Fota Wildlife Park, offering the visitor a change of pace from the predominance of water and sea. Between Cork and Youghal, the small town of Midleton boasts one of the*

oldest distilleries in Ireland, Jameson, home to the famous Irish whiskey. The equally well known Blarney Castle, with its "magic" stone, is only a short trip to the north of Cork. To the south, Kinsale is a charming fishing village full of places to eat and its fair share of comfortable accommodation, making it a good base for exploring the area.

Blarney Castle

🔟 Sights

1. Cork City
2. Kinsale
3. Cobh
4. Youghal
5. Blarney Castle
6. Fota Wildlife Park
7. Timoleague Abbey
8. Old Midleton Distillery
9. Charles Fort
10. Royal Gunpowder Mills

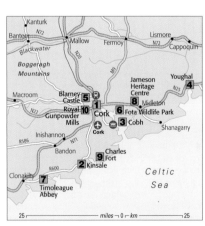

Cork City

Officially Ireland's second city, built on either side of the River Lee, Cork is a true rival to Dublin according to the local residents, of which there are around 120,000. The picturesque quays both north and south of the river, linked by an array of bridges, offer spectacular views. The numerous waterways, narrow alleys and Georgian buildings, together with the balmy climate, often lend the city a more continental than Irish atmosphere. ® Map Q3

Kinsale

The fact that Kinsale has its own gourmet food festival gives some idea of the calibre of restaurants and cafés here. It is probably the most prosperous and sophisticated fishing village in the country and, being only 27 km (17 miles) from Cork city, attracts locals and tourists in droves. The pretty harbour is the focal point and most of the activity centres on this area and the backstreets around it. ® Map Q3

Cobh

Pronounced "Cove", this 19th-century town boasts one of the world's largest natural harbours. In its heyday, the town was a major commercial sea port as well as being the stopover port for luxury passenger liners,

Kinsale

Youghal

including the *Sirius*, which made her maiden voyage from here. Cobh was also the last port of call for the *Titanic* before she sailed to her tragic end. The Queenstown Story is an interesting exhibition detailing the town's maritime history. Particularly poignant is the section on the part Cobh played in the transportation of convicts to Australia in the 18th and 19th centuries. ® Map Q3 • The Queenstown Story: Cobh Heritage Centre; 021 481 3591; Open May–Oct: 9:30am–6pm Mon–Sat, 11am–6pm Sun; Nov–Apr: 9:30am–5pm Mon–Sat; Dis. access, Adm

Youghal

About 50 km (31 miles) east of Cork city, Youghal (pronounced "Yawl") has a great location on both the Atlantic Ocean and the tamer banks of the River Blackwater's estuary. The impressive walls enclosing the town were built by the English to protect the village from attack by the native Irish. Queen Elizabeth I bestowed Youghal on Sir Walter Raleigh in gratitude for faithful service. Under Cromwell, however, the town became an English Protestant garrison. ® Map Q4

Old Midleton Distillery

Blarney Castle

It is really the Blarney Stone, believed to have been gifted to the King of Munster by Robert the Bruce, that brings visitors flocking here. Legend has it that whoever kisses the stone will be given the gift of eloquent speech. The castle itself dates from the mid-15th century and the Banqueting Hall and Great Hall are fine examples of the architecture of the period.
§ *Blarney* • *021 4385252* • *Map Q3* • *Open daily* • *Dis. access* • *Adm*

Fota Wildlife Park

This 75-acre centre prides itself on helping to protect the environment, breeding and reintroducing animals to their natural habitats. Its cheetah-breeding programme is the most successful in the world, outside of Africa, with 180 cubs born since 1984. § *Carrigtwohill, Cobh* • *021 481 2678* • *Map Q3* • *Open 10am–5pm Mon–Sat, 10:30am–5pm Sun* • *Dis. access* • *Adm*

Blarney Stone, Blarney Castle

Timoleague Abbey

A bleak atmosphere presides here, when the mist hangs over the shore and the ruined 13th-century Franciscan abbey sits broodingly on the waterside. Of particular interest is the wine cellar – the friars prospered on the importation of Spanish wines in the 16th century. § *Timoleague* • *Map R3* • *Open daily* • *Free*

Old Midleton Distillery

An excellent audiovisual presentation of the story of Jameson Irish Whiskey, with a tour of the still houses, a distiller's cottage, mills and maltings, and a popular whiskey tasting. § *Midleton* • *021 4613594* • *Map Q3* • *Open daily* • *Adm*

Charles Fort

Built in the late 17th century, Charles Fort has been associated with some of the most important events in Irish history, including the Williamite War of 1689–1691 and the Irish Civil War in 1922–23. § *Summer Cove, Kinsale* • *021 477 2263* • *Map Q3* • *Open Nov–mid-Mar: 10am–5pm daily; mid-Mar–Oct: 10am–6pm* • *Adm*

Royal Gunpowder Mills

Gunpowder was one of Cork's most important industries in the mid-19th century until the mills closed in 1903. Visitors can see the canals, sluices, weirs, mills and workers' cottages.
§ *Ballincollig* • *Map Q3* • *Dis. access*

Price Categories

For a three-course	€	under €35
meal for one with half	€€	€35–€45
a bottle of wine (or	€€€	€45–€65
equivalent meal), taxes	€€€€	€65–€90
and extra charges.	€€€€€	over €90

Above **Ballymaloe House**

Places to Eat and Drink

1 Aherne's Seafood Restaurant and Bar

This popular, relaxed restaurant, serving delicious fresh seafood dishes, brings people from miles around. 🚫 *163 N Main St, Youghal • Map Q4 • 024 92424 • Dis. access • €€*

2 Café Paradiso

This delightful restaurant serves a truly elegant menu of inventive vegetarian cuisine made from quality ingredients. The presentation is excellent and the staff are wonderful. 🚫 *16 Lancaster Quay • Map Q3 • 021 427 7939 • €€€*

3 Blair's Inn

This award-winning bar-restaurant is full of nooks and crannies, with open fires in winter and a beer garden in summer. The speciality is local, seasonal fare: try O'Flynn's gourmet pork and leek sausages. 🚫 *Cloghroe, Blarney, Co Cork • Map Q3 • 021 438 1470 • €€*

4 Longueville House

An elegant country house hotel with delicious dining in rather grand surrounds. The owners produce their own apple brandy, garden berry liqueurs and cider, and coffee comes with handmade chocolates. 🚫 *Mallow, Co. Cork • Map Q3 • 022 47156 • €€€€€*

5 Isaacs

Very popular with locals and visitors, the unpretentious food is consistently good. 🚫 *48 MacCurtain St, Cork • Map Q3 • 021 450 3805 • Closed Sun lunch • Dis. access • €€€*

6 Ballymaloe House

Darina and Tim Allen's cookery school held here has a worldwide reputation and it is hardly surprising that the food is absolutely delicious. Booking is essential. 🚫 *Shanagarry • Map Q3 • 021 465 2531 • Dis. access • €€€*

7 Malt House Granary

Located in the town centre, this restaurant offers friendly, knowledgeable service and a wide range of West Cork culinary specialities. 🚫 *30 Ashe St, Clonakilty, Co Cork • Map Q3 • 023 883 4355 • €*

8 An Súgan

An extremely popular pub. The West Cork creamy chowder is a hit with the locals. 🚫 *41 Wolf Tone St, Clonakilty • Map Q3 • 023 883 3719 • Dis. access • €€*

9 Crackpots

Eating here is an interesting experience because you are surrounded by unusual artwork and pottery – hence the name. The food is an equally unusual mix of styles and flavours and the atmosphere is relaxed and informal. 🚫 *3 Cork St, Kinsale • Map Q3 • 021 477 2847 • €€*

10 Fishy Fishy Café

This very popular café is right beside the pretty harbour in the fishing village of Kinsale. It's no surprise that delicious seafood is always available. 🚫 *Pier Rd, Kinsale • Map Q3 • 021 470 0415 • Dis. access • €€€*

Note: *Unless otherwise stated, all restaurants accept credit cards and serve vegetarian meals*

Left **Rock of Cashel** Right **Limerick**

Tipperary, Limerick and Clare

FROM THE LUSH GREENERY OF TIPPERARY *to the traffic jams of Limerick, and from the leisurely vacation boats cruising on the wide river Shannon up to the stark, stirring emptiness of The Burren, this region embraces the full diversity of rural Ireland. There are scores of impressive historic sights and picture-perfect villages, as well as unpretentious country towns with not a tourist in sight. Cross the Shannon to reach the rockier majesty of County Clare, whose rural way of life retains a profound simplicity and sense of independence. Culturally, it is rooted in tradition, and you'll hear plenty of Irish music played in village pubs. Clare's coastline rises in dramatic cliffs that take the force of the Atlantic, while inland, wind-battered gorse and bracken are broken up by high pasture. Sheep wander unfenced, walking over the hills and along the country lanes as if all this land were theirs.*

Cliffs of Moher

🔟 Sights

1. Cashel
2. Limerick
3. Cliffs of Moher
4. The Burren
5. River Shannon
6. Kilrush and Loop Head Drive
7. Bunratty Castle
8. Foynes Flying Boat Museum
9. Ennis
10. Killaloe

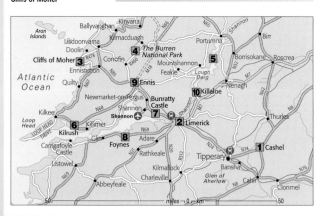

Cashel

This quiet country town is dominated by the awesome Rock of Cashel, topped by stone structures known in pre-Christian times as Cashel of Kings (from Gaelic *caiseal*, a stone fortress). Sensing the rising power of the church, in 1101 the Kings of Munster re-defined themselves as a dynasty of royal archbishops and built great ecclesiastical buildings. Most were destroyed by the English in 1647, but highlights of what survives are: 12th-century Cormac's Chapel, the earliest Romanesque church in Ireland; the roofless 13th-century cathedral; and the 15th-century Vicars' Choral, the residential quarters of the cathedral cantors.
◈ *Cashel • Map N2*

Limerick

A grim portrait of industrial Limerick, the third-largest city in the republic, was painted by Frank McCourt's novel *Angela's Ashes (see p35)*. It's not that bad now. The city centre has good restaurants and pubs and a pleasant atmosphere. Historical sights include the imposing King John's Castle. Built in 1210, the castle is home to a display on the town's 800-year history and the Hunt Museum, with its magnificent collection of Irish antiquities. ◈ *Map P3 • King John's Castle: Open Apr–Sep: 9:30am–5:30pm; (Oct–Nov: till 4:30pm); Adm • Hunt Museum: Rutland St; Open 10am–5pm Mon–Sat, 2–5pm Sun; Adm*

Cliffs of Moher

Five miles (8 km) of sheer cliffs rising as much as 702 ft (214 m) up from the pounding Atlantic, this is one of Europe's grandest stretches of coastline. Take the cliff-edge footpath round to O'Brien's Tower, which gives a stunning view. ◈ *Map N2 • Visitors' Centre, Liscannor, Co Clare: Open from 9am daily; 065 708 6141; Adm*

The Burren

A weird limestone desert of flat rock "pavements", at first glance most of the 100-sq-mile (260-sq-km) Burren (pronounced "burn") seems lifeless. But the web of hidden gulleys is brimming with plants, some very rare. Once densely populated, the Burren preserves dolmens, ruined towers and ring-forts. Visit the Burren Centre to learn more. ◈ *Map N2 • Burren Centre: Kilfenora; Open Mar–May & Sep–Oct: 10am–5pm daily; Jun–Aug: 9:30am–5:30pm daily; 065 708 8030; Adm*

The Burren

5 River Shannon

Ireland's longest river opens into broad lakes, eventually widening into a huge estuary. The river's curve traditionally marks the border of the west. Lough Derg, the largest lake is a popular area for boating and angling. ❧ *Map P2*

6 Kilrush and Loop Head Drive

While Kilrush itself is unremarkable, it makes a good base for exploring the furthest reaches of southwest County Clare. Especially worthwhile is a drive out to remote Loop Head. For an insight into local history, particularly the hardships under English rule, visit the Kilrush Heritage Centre. A must-see is the Walled Garden of the Vandeleur Family Demesne. ❧ *Map P2 • Kilrush Heritage Centre: Open Apr–Sep: 10am–5pm Mon–Fri, 1–5pm Sun; Oct–Mar: 10am–4pm Mon–Fri • Adm*

7 Bunratty Castle

The sturdy 15th-century stronghold of the O'Briens, Earls of Thomond, has become the top venue for mock medieval banquets and other entertainment. The five-storey structure was fully restored by Viscount Gort in 1954. Behind the castle, Bunratty Folk

Banqueting room, Bunratty Castle

Burren Botany

Apart from seasonal pools, called *turloughs*, the Burren's limestone does not hold water. Yet more than 1,100 plant species thrive here, because countless cracks in the rocks and stones accumulate organic matter and provide shelter. Especially common are mosses, lichens, rock rose, mountain avens, orchids and bloody cranesbill.

Park gives insight into traditional rural culture. ❧ *Bunratty • 061 360788 • Map P3 • Open 9:30am–5:30pm daily; Last adm to castle 4pm • Adm*

8 Foynes Flying Boat Museum

Transatlantic flights between Ireland and the US began in Foynes in 1939, and in 1942 the first nonstop passenger flights between Europe and America started here. The museum tells the story. There is also a 1940s-style tearoom. ❧ *Foynes • Map P2 • Open mid-Mar–May: 9:30am–5pm, Jun–Sep: 9am–6pm • Adm*

9 Ennis

This likeable little town, with its bright shopfronts and music pubs, first grew up in the 13th century around the Franciscan community of Ennis Friary. Shut down in 1692, the abbey fell into ruin but what survives – mostly 15th-century – includes the richly carved MacMahon Tomb. ❧ *Map P2 • Friary: 065 6829100; Open Apr–Sep: 10am–6pm, Oct: 10am–5pm; Dis. access; Adm*

10 Killaloe

A chic marina town rising steeply from the southern end of Lough Derg, Killaloe is a centre for watersports. Its 12th-century St Flannan's Cathedral and Oratory have Romanesque decorative stonework. ❧ *Map P3*

Price Categories

For a three-course meal for one with half a bottle of wine (or equivalent meal), taxes and extra charges.	€ under €35
	€€ €35–€45
	€€€ €45–€65
	€€€€ €65–€90
	€€€€€ over €90

Above **The Mustard Seed**

🔟 Places to Eat

1 Copper and Spice
A stylish restaurant that presents both Indian and Asian cuisine, with lots of good options for vegetarians. Service is warm and prices are very reasonable.
🚇 *2 Cornmarket Row, Limerick • Map P3 • 061 313620 • Dis. access • €*

2 Durty Nelly's Oyster Restaurant
This mellow village inn, in the shadow of Bunratty Castle, has been in business since 1620, and still serves a range of substantial Irish dishes, oysters and seafood. 🚇 *Bunratty • Map P3 • 061 364861 • Dis. access • €€*

3 Earl of Thomond
This aristocratic room at Dromoland Castle is the perfect place for a lavish lunch or dinner after a day on the adjoining golf course. 🚇 *Newmarket on Fergus • Map P3 • 061 368144 • €€€€*

4 Barrtra Seafood Restaurant
This cliff-side, bay-facing cottage is an institution, offering a singular atmosphere, a kind welcome and wonderful seafood. 🚇 *Miltown Malbay Rd, Lahinch, Co. Clare • Map P3 • 065 708 1280 • Opening times vary • €€€*

5 Molly's Bar and Restaurant
A pub-style restaurant on the shores of Lough Derg, Molly's serves simply cooked, fresh local produce. 🚇 *Ballina, Killaloe • Map P3 • 061 376632 • Dis. access • €*

6 Cherry Tree Restaurant
A County Clare favourite thanks to its consistently good cooking and pretty Shannon-side views. Enjoy dishes like fillet of beef, Bluebell Falls goat's cheese or slow-roasted pork belly.
🚇 *Lakeside, Ballina Killaloe • Map P3 • 061 375688 • Dis. access • €€€*

7 Linnanes Lobster Bar
Stunning views of the Burren and Aughinish Island complement the delicious seafood on offer.
🚇 *The Pier, New Quay, Co Clare • Map N2 • 065 707 8120 • Dis. access • €€*

8 The Mustard Seed
This bustling restaurant within a Victorian country house hotel offers fine modern Irish cuisine and an excellent wine list. Stylish, but not pretentious.
🚇 *Echo Lodge, Ballingarry • Map P3 • 069 68508 • Dis. access • €€€*

9 The Arches
This is an affordable, family-run eatery in the centre of one of Ireland's prettiest villages and is well known for its hearty home cooking and friendly service. 🚇 *Adare • Map P3 • 061 396246 • Dis. access • €€*

10 Cullinans
This family-owned restaurant (and guesthouse) in the centre of Doolin village is renowned for its speciality of locally caught and simply prepared fresh seafood.
🚇 *Doolin • Map P3 • 065 707 4183 • Open Easter–Oct • Dis. access • €€*

Note: *Unless otherwise stated, all restaurants accept credit cards and serve vegetarian meals*

Left **Clonmacnoise ruins** Right **Kilbeggan Distillery**

Clonmacnoise and the Midlands

1 Clonmacnoise

This early Christian site, founded by St Ciaran in the 6th century, draws tourists into Ireland's often neglected Midlands. The grounds are atmospheric, especially on a grey Irish day, and include the ruins of a cathedral, seven churches (10th–13th-centuries), two round towers, three high crosses and dozens of early Christian grave slabs. The visitors' centre offers an audiovisual show and exhibitions. ◈ *Shannonbridge • 0909 674195 • Map N4 • Open mid-Mar–May, Sep & Oct: 10am–6pm; Jun–Aug: 9am–6:30pm; Nov–mid-Mar: 10am–5:30pm • Dis. access (visitors' centre) • Adm*

2 Birr Castle, Gardens and Telescope

It's rare that a castle plays second fiddle to its surroundings. Here, however, the gardens, covering more than 123 acres of parkland and containing 2,000 species of rare trees and shrubs, take the prize. Spring blossoms and autumn foliage are mesmerizing. The grounds are also home to the Earl of Rosse's 180-cm (72-inch) telescope. Built in the 1840s this was once the world's largest. ◈ *Birr • 05791 20336 • Map N4 • Open mid-Mar–Oct: 10am–6pm; Nov–mid-Mar: 10am–4pm • Dis. access • Adm*

3 Emo Court

Designed in 1790 for the Earl of Portarlington, this is another fine example of architect James Gandon's work, and his interiors in this lovely house remain

Emo Court

unchanged. The fine gardens are divided into two sections: the Grapery leads you down to a lakeside walk; the Clucker acquired its name from the nuns who used to reside here. ◈ *Portlaoise • 057 8626 573 • Map N4 • House: Open Easter–Sep: 10am–6pm; Gardens: Open dawn–dusk daily • Adm to house*

4 The Kilbeggan Distillery Experience

Originally known as Locke's, the distillery closed in 1957, a full two centuries after getting its licence in 1757. It has now been restored as a museum, displaying original 1920s machinery and offering an intriguing glimpse into the lives of the people who worked there. Visitors receive a complimentary sample of Kilbeggan Irish Whiskey at the end of the guided tour. ◈ *Kilbeggan, Co. Westmeath • 057 933 2134 • Map N4 • Open Apr–Oct: 9am–6pm; Nov–Mar: 10am–4pm • Adm*

5 Birr

Although largely dominated by the castle and its grounds, the town of Birr has much to

offer visitors. Its beautiful Georgian style has been lovingly preserved, with many of the buildings retaining their original fanlights and door panelling.
🕲 *Map N4*

Rock of Dunamase
Towering 45 m (150 ft) above a flat plain, the Rock of Dunamase is one of the most impressive and historic sights in Ireland. The sight was included on Ptolemy's world map in AD 140, such was its fame, and the ruins date back thousands of years. Standing amid its history, you can see all the way to the Slieve Bloom Mountains. 🕲 *Laois • Map N4*

Belvedere House
Despite a perfect Austen-style setting, there was no sense or sensibility in the actions of the Earl of Belvedere. He began the house in 1740, spent his life fighting his brothers and built the Gothic Jealous Wall to block the view of his sibling's house. He also imprisoned his wife for 31 years, suspecting she'd slept with one of them. Visitors, however, are free to roam the beautiful gardens and the shore of Lough Ennell. 🕲 *N52, Mullingar • 044 394 9060 • Map N4 • Open 7 days a week, all year • Dis. access • Adm*

Tullynally Castle
Constructed in the 17th century, most of Tullynally today is a result of the second Earl of Longford's remodelling of it as a Gothic Revival castle, housing a collection of Irish furniture and portraits. Outside are romantic grounds and walled gardens.
🕲 *Castlepollard • Map M4 • 044 966 1159 • Castle: Open to groups by arrangement; Gardens: Open May–Sep: 11am–6pm Thu–Sun • Adm*

Slieve Bloom Mountains
Despite only rising 527 m (1,729 ft), the surrounding flat plain aids in creating an imposing image of the Slieve Bloom Mountains. The summits have been declared a National Nature Reserve and the Slieve Bloom Way has been marked out for hikers who have waterfalls and hidden glens to look forward to.
🕲 *Map N4*

Bog of Allen
Once the largest raised peat bog in Ireland, the bog has been gradually shrinking as it is used for powering the island. It is home to some of Ireland's most interesting indigenous plants and insects, including the carnivorous sundew plant. 🕲 *Bog of Allen Nature Centre, Lullymore • 045 860133 • Map N5*

Rock of Dunamase

Left **Galway** Right **Lough Corrib**

Around Galway

COUNTY GALWAY HAS A PECULIAR MAJESTY *and an awesome sense of its closeness to nature, stalwartly facing the imposing Atlantic Ocean. Even the area around the county town, Galway City, squeezed onto a strip of land between the expanse of Lough Corrib and the immense waters of Galway Bay, possesses that same inspiring quality. As well as its own charms, with good restaurants and charming pubs, it is a good base from which to explore the area. South of the city is a gentler, greener countryside. While a good deal of the fascination of this southern edge of Galway lies simply in*

the tranquil landscape, for lovers of literature much of the interest is also in the connection with the romantic Irish poet WB Yeats (see p34). Although not originally from this region, Yeats returned often in his thoughts and in his work to the myths and grandeur of western Ireland, and spent many years living at his Thoor Ballylee near Gort, south of Galway City. Pleasant, gentle cruises on the lakes are another attraction.

Kinvarra

🔟 Sights

1. Galway City
2. Lough Corrib
3. Kinvarra
4. Coole Park
5. Cong Abbey
6. Oughterard
7. Thoor Ballylee
8. Kilmacduagh Monastery
9. Spiddal
10. Athenry

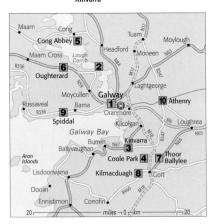

Galway City

Coole Park
The woods, lakes and paths of this national park and wildlife preserve, with its red deer and red squirrels, were once the grounds of a great Georgian mansion, home of Lady Augusta Gregory. She hosted the most famous novelists and playwrights of her day and the Irish Revival began here. Names carved on the Autograph Tree include Shaw, Synge, Sean O'Casey and many more. The house itself fell into ruin and was dismantled. ❧ *Gort • Map N3 • Open end-Apr–Jun, Sep: 10am–5pm daily; Jun–Aug: 10am-6pm • Free • www.coolepark.ie*

Galway City
The pleasant, bustling regional capital started life as a fortress of the O'Connors of Connacht. Colonized in 1235 by Anglo-Normans, it became a prosperous seaport: some fine buildings survive, notably 16th-century Lynch's Castle (now a bank), and 14th-century St Nicholas's Church. A great atmosphere, with plenty of music and traditional shops. ❧ *Map N2*

Cong Abbey
Poised on the narrow strip between Lough Corrib and Lough Mask, the attractive village of Cong lies just across the Galway border in County Mayo. Cong Abbey was an important Augustinian community founded by the King of Connacht in 1120 and became a leading spiritual centre. Closed down during the Reformation, it fell into ruin. What survives remains majestic; the cloisters have been partly reconstructed. ❧ *Cong • Map M2*

Lough Corrib
The vast expanse of Lough Corrib's cool waters, feeling more like part of the Atlantic Ocean than a lake, is Ireland's second largest, and a popular resort area for angling, boating and walking. ❧ *Map N2*

Kinvara
The little road around Galway Bay passes through a score of villages that are breathtaking in their prettiness and grandiose location. The most charming is Kinvarra, with its fishing harbour and pier cottages. It's the setting for a traditional music festival in May, and a Gathering of the Boats festival in August. ❧ *Map N3*

Doorway, Cong Abbey

6 Oughterard

On the shores of Lough Corrib, this village has become a small resort area. Its chief prize, however, is Aughnanure Castle, beside the lake – a handsome remnant of a 16th-century tower-house of the O'Flaherty clan of Connacht who terrorized the ruling Anglo-Norman families of Galway. ✪ Map N2 • Aughnanure Castle: Open Apr–Oct: 9:30am–6pm daily • Adm

7 Thoor Ballylee

Follow the sign "Yeats Tower" to reach the old towerhouse in which WB Yeats and his wife Georgie spent much time during the 1920s. A sturdy little fortress, it was restored and converted by Yeats, and is described with touching detail in many of his poems. The house was damaged by flooding in 2009 and is presently closed – call for details. ✪ Gort • 091 537 700 • Map N3

8 Kilmacduagh Monastery

An astonishing set of monastic ruins survives here. The original church established in AD 610 was enlarged over the centuries and replaced by a cathedral in the 11th or 12th century, though keeping many

Thoor Ballylee

features of the older buildings, including an 11th-century door. Around it are a number of other intriguing 13th- and 14th-century ecclesiastical buildings. There's also a Leaning Tower. ✪ Gort • Map N3

9 Spiddal

Officially Irish-speaking, and with a Gaelic summer school, Spiddal makes a pleasant stop on the Galway Bay coast road. Several craft workers have set up shop in the Spiddal Craft Village, where you can see pottery, weaving, knitting and other skilled work in progress, and buy the finished goods. ✪ Map N2

10 Athenry

The poignant folksong "The Fields of Athenry" (pronounced Athen-rye) gives little clue about this evocative reminder of the Anglo-Norman colonists. In 1235, Meiler de Bermingham was granted a charter to Athenry, where he built a little castle, and founded a Dominican Priory in 1241 where he and his descendants could be buried. Today, though damaged, much survives, together with a broken 15th-century cross erected in the central square. ✪ Map N3

To Be Carved

One of Yeats's poems is entitled *To Be Carved on a Stone at Thoor Ballylee*, and the words have indeed been carved at the house:
"I, the poet William Yeats
With old mill boards and sea-green slates
And smithy work from the Gorge forge
Restored this tower for my wife George;
And may these characteristics remain
When all is ruin once again".

Above **Ard Bia at Nimmos**

🔟 Places to Eat

1 Pins Gastro Bar
This eatery serves modern Irish cuisine with an emphasis on local suppliers. Try wild mullet and Connemara lamb. ❧ *The Twelve Hotel, Barna Village, Galway • Map N2 • 091 597000 • €€*

2 Cre na Cille
Seafood, meat and game are the specialities of this excellent but unassuming family-run restaurant. It also has a large array of fine whiskeys. ❧ *High St, Tuam • Map N2 • 093 28232 • Open Tue–Sat • €€€*

3 Paddy Burke's Oyster Inn
The best time to visit this traditional pub is during Clarinbridge's September oyster festival. As well as shellfish from the famed local beds, it offers a choice of good meat and fish dishes. ❧ *Clarinbridge • Map N2 • 091 796226 • Dis. access • €*

4 The Seafood Bar @ Kirwan's Lane
A pretty two-storey restaurant serving creative cuisine with a modern Irish theme, such as linguine of fresh langoustines and clams. ❧ *Kirwan's Lane, Galway • Map N3 • 091 568266 • €€€*

5 Ard Bia at Nimmos
Restaurant, café, art gallery – this reputable eatery offers a delicious menu with Irish, European and Middle Eastern influences. Try Colleran's spiced lamb borek. ❧ *Spanish Arch, Galway City • Map N2 • 091 561114 • €€*

6 Cashel House
This country house and restaurant was once a gracious aristocratic home and has now earned itself international renown for both its food and atmosphere. ❧ *Cashel • Map N2 • 095 31001 • €€€€*

7 O'Dowd's Seafood Bar and Restaurant
Beside Roundstone's pretty harbour, O'Dowd's serves steak and seafood dishes and does more for vegetarians than most Irish restaurants. ❧ *Roundstone • Map N1 • 095 35809 • €€*

8 Aran Islands Hotel
Modern Irish cuisine is served in the cosy surroundings of the restaurant and bar of this island hotel overlooking Kilronan Harbour and Killeaney Bay. ❧ *Kilronan, Inis Mór, Aran Islands • Map N2 • 099 61104 • Dis. access • €*

9 White Gables
In an informal whitewashed 19th-century inn, White Gables is best known for its lobster, but also serves other "surf and turf" dishes. ❧ *Moycullen Village • Map N2 • 091 555744 • €€€*

10 McDonagh's Seafood House
As you might expect, specializing mainly in seafood. Excellent seafood platter and friendly service. ❧ *22 Quay St, Galway City • Map N3 • 091 565001 • €€*

Note: Unless otherwise stated, all restaurants accept credit cards and serve vegetarian meals

Left **Clifden Bay** Right **Connemara National Park**

Connemara and Mayo

ONNEMARA – THE ROCKY, MOUNTAINOUS COUNTRYSIDE *of western County Galway – is largely uncultivated, a strange wilderness of water and stone, peat bog, headlands and barren hills. Along its shores, the Atlantic eats savagely into the land, making spectacular inlets and bays. Seemingly uninhabitable, in pre-famine days Connemara was crowded with poverty-stricken farmers, victims of the Protestant Ascendancy that had driven them from their farms across the Shannon. Thousands of rough dry-stone walls criss-cross the bare hills, enclosing their tiny abandoned fields. The famine wiped out most of Connemara's population, and the memory of that disaster lingers sadly in the glorious landscape. The poignant scenery continues across Killary Fjord into County Mayo, where – as well as wide open spaces of bog, heath, mountain and lake – there are appealing small towns, a traditional way of life, and much to see.*

Detail, Westport House

🔟 Sights

1. Westport
2. Clifden
3. Kylemore Abbey
4. Connemara National Park and Twelve Bens Mountains
5. Sky Road
6. Roundstone
7. Leenane to Killary Harbour
8. Clare and Inishbofin Islands
9. Croagh Patrick
10. Céide Fields

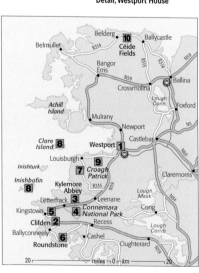

Price Categories

For a three-course
meal for one with half
a bottle of wine (or
equivalent meal), taxes
and extra charges.

€ under €35
€€ €35–€45
€€€ €45–€65
€€€€ €65–€90
€€€€€ over €90

Above **Ard Bia at Nimmos**

🔟 Places to Eat

Pins Gastro Bar
This eatery serves modern Irish cuisine with an emphasis on local suppliers. Try wild mullet and Connemara lamb. ⌦ *The Twelve Hotel, Barna Village, Galway • Map N2* • 091 597000 • €€

Cre na Cille
Seafood, meat and game are the specialities of this excellent but unassuming family-run restaurant. It also has a large array of fine whiskeys. ⌦ *High St, Tuam • Map N2* • 093 28232 • Open Tue–Sat • €€€

Paddy Burke's Oyster Inn
The best time to visit this traditional pub is during Clarinbridge's September oyster festival. As well as shellfish from the famed local beds, it offers a choice of good meat and fish dishes. ⌦ *Clarinbridge • Map N2* • 091 796226 • Dis. access • €

The Seafood Bar @ Kirwan's Lane
A pretty two-storey restaurant serving creative cuisine with a modern Irish theme, such as linguine of fresh langoustines and clams. ⌦ *Kirwan's Lane, Galway • Map N3 • 091 568266 • €€€*

Ard Bia at Nimmos
Restaurant, café, art gallery – this reputable eatery offers a delicious menu with Irish, European and Middle Eastern influences. Try Colleran's spiced lamb borek. ⌦ *Spanish Arch, Galway City • Map N2 • 091 561114 • €€*

Cashel House
This country house and restaurant was once a gracious aristocratic home and has now earned itself international renown for both its food and atmosphere. ⌦ *Cashel • Map N2* • 095 31001 • €€€€

O'Dowd's Seafood Bar and Restaurant
Beside Roundstone's pretty harbour, O'Dowd's serves steak and seafood dishes and does more for vegetarians than most Irish restaurants. ⌦ *Roundstone • Map N1 • 095 35809 • €€*

Aran Islands Hotel
Modern Irish cuisine is served in the cosy surroundings of the restaurant and bar of this island hotel overlooking Kilronan Harbour and Killeaney Bay. ⌦ *Kilronan, Inis Mór, Aran Islands • Map N2 • 099 61104 • Dis. access • €*

White Gables
In an informal whitewashed 19th-century inn, White Gables is best known for its lobster, but also serves other "surf and turf" dishes. ⌦ *Moycullen Village • Map N2* • 091 555744 • €€€

McDonagh's Seafood House
As you might expect, specializing mainly in seafood. Excellent seafood platter and friendly service. ⌦ *22 Quay St, Galway City • Map N3 • 091 565001 • €€*

 Note: Unless otherwise stated, all restaurants accept credit cards and serve vegetarian meals

Left **Clifden Bay** Right **Connemara National Park**

Connemara and Mayo

CONNEMARA – THE ROCKY, MOUNTAINOUS COUNTRYSIDE *of western County Galway – is largely uncultivated, a strange wilderness of water and stone, peat bog, headlands and barren hills. Along its shores, the Atlantic eats savagely into the land, making spectacular inlets and bays. Seemingly uninhabitable, in pre-famine days Connemara was crowded with poverty-stricken farmers, victims of the Protestant Ascendancy that had driven them from their farms across the Shannon. Thousands of rough dry-stone walls criss-cross the bare hills, enclosing their tiny abandoned fields. The famine wiped out most of Connemara's population, and the memory of that disaster lingers sadly in the glorious landscape. The poignant scenery continues across Killary Fjord into County Mayo, where – as well as wide open spaces of bog, heath, mountain and lake – there are appealing small towns, a traditional way of life, and much to see.*

Detail, Westport House

Sights

1. Westport
2. Clifden
3. Kylemore Abbey
4. Connemara National Park and Twelve Bens Mountains
5. Sky Road
6. Roundstone
7. Leenane to Killary Harbour
8. Clare and Inishbofin Islands
9. Croagh Patrick
10. Céide Fields

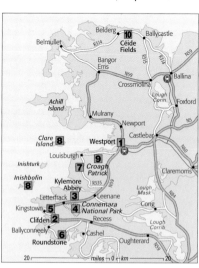

Westport

Busy, popular Westport is still small enough that countryside can be seen at the end of the main streets. Originally built in 1780 by the Earl of Altamont as an adjunct to his mansion, Westport House, this is a good example of a planned town, with its dignified central Octagon and tree-lined Mall. It was all paid for by the slave-worked West Indian sugar plantations of the Earl's wife. Westport House remains imposing and grandly furnished, although touristy, with added attractions such as a pirate adventure park for children.
Map M2 • Westport House: Open Mar–Oct: 10am–4pm (times vary); Adm

Clifden

Regarded as the "capital" of Connemara, although hardly more than a village, this busy little resort lies among lovely green hills above Clifden Bay and at the foot of the Twelve Bens Mountains. A Georgian planned town built by John d'Arcy, it retains a certain character and style. At the end of summer, Clifden hosts the traditional Connemara Pony Show, which brings in hordes of horse-lovers.
Map M1

Kylemore Abbey

The extraordinarily over-elaborate mock Gothic castle, built as a private house in 1868 for millionaire Mitchell Henry, has been a Benedictine convent since the 1920s. Although a religious community, it is also run as a commercial tourist attraction. The house and walled gardens are delightful and the location magnificent, next to Kylemore Lough and with views towards the Twelve Bens.
Kylemore • 095 52001 • Map M2 • Open daylight hours daily • Adm

Connemara National Park and Twelve Bens Mountains

Extending from Letterfrack village to the Twelve Bens, the park is a 7,300-acre conservation area of heath, bog and hills encompassing the grandest of Connemara's landscapes. The Twelve Bens, a dozen high peaks rising from the heart of the western mountains, dominate the Connemara skyline. A visitors' centre near the park entrance has a permanent exhibition on the flora, fauna, geology and history of the region. *Map M2 • Visitors' Centre: Letterfrack; 095 41054; Open 9am–5:30pm daily; Free*

Kylemore Abbey

Grace O'Malley

Grace O'Malley (1530–1603) was the daughter of a Connacht chieftain. At 15, she married the O'Flaherty chief, whose men remained loyal to her after his death. With fortresses throughout Connacht, and based on Clare Island, in 1593 she visited Queen Elizabeth I, extracting a promise to be left in peace.

5 Sky Road

Named for its beautiful cliff-edge ocean views, the Sky Road is a 11-km (7-mile) loop that starts out from Clifden to skirt the narrow peninsula alongside Clifden Bay. Along the way it reaches empty beaches, wild hill scenery, and sights such as the ruins of Neo-Gothic Clifden Castle, the home of Clifden's founder John d'Arcy. ✎ *Map M1*

6 Roundstone

Cloch na Rón is the official name of this attractively laid out, Irish-speaking "planned village" built in the 1820s. In one way, it's an authentic, unpretentious lobster-fishing community, but it also has an arty side and many attractions for visitors, including a good beach, a range of eating places, galleries and traditional shops. ✎ *Map N2*

7 Leenane to Killary Harbour

The appealing village of Leenane lies beside the long, narrow inlet of Killary Fjord. From here, the dramatically beautiful road to the small oceanside resort of Louisburgh crosses the water between the peaks of Devil's Mother and Ben Gorm, and rises among lakes and streams along the narrow Delphi Valley, in places bursting with rhododendrons. One of the west's loveliest drives. ✎ *Map M2*

8 Clare and Inishbofin Islands

Dramatic Clare Island was the stronghold of Grace O'Malley, or Granuaile, whose little fortress still stands, as does the ruined abbey where she is buried. Inishbofin has a green, lonely beauty. Home of the O'Flaherty clan and a hideaway of Grace O'Malley, it was taken by Cromwell. Both islands have small populations and prehistoric ruins. ✎ *Map M1*

9 Croagh Patrick

This is one of Ireland's most sacred sites. St Patrick fasted on the summit for 40 days in AD 441. It is considered a pious act to make the steep climb on the rough, cutting stones to the summit (which gives phenomenal views). On Reek Sunday, the last Sunday in July, over 25,000 pilgrims visit, and many ascend in bare feet. ✎ *Map M2*

10 Céide Fields

Preserved for thousands of years under a blanket of peat bog, the Céide site consists of Stone Age walled fields, together with stone ruins. Excellent guided tours are offered by the visitors' centre. ✎ *Map L2* • Open Apr–May & Oct: 10am–5pm daily (Jun–Sep until 6pm) • Adm

Croagh Patrick

Price Categories

For a three-course	€ under €35
meal for one with half	€€ €35–€45
a bottle of wine (or	€€€ €45–€65
equivalent meal), taxes	€€€€ €65–€90
and extra charges.	€€€€€ over €90

Above **Renvyle House**

🔟 Places to Eat

1 Mitchell's
A family-style restaurant in the Connemara village of Clifden, serving comforting, home-style food, such as seafood and poultry dishes, in a relaxed setting. ✎ *Market St, Clifden, Co. Galway • Map M1 • 095 21867 • €€*

2 Burke's Bar & Restaurant
This lively pub in the village of Clonbur serves meat, fish and poultry dishes as well as home-baked scones and soda bread. Outside dining in summer. ✎ *Mount Gable House, Clonbur, Co. Galway • Map N3 • 094 9546175 • Dis. access • €€*

3 Renvyle House
A gracious country house-style hotel on the shores of the Atlantic serving superb seafood, Connemara lamb, and a range of other classic Irish and European dishes. Booking is advisable. ✎ *Renvyle • Map M1 • 095 46100 • Dis. access • €€€*

4 JW Brasserie
Award-winning contemporary Irish restaurant, popular with locals and tourists alike. ✎ *The Octagon, Westport, Co. Mayo • Map M2 • 098 25027 • Dis. access • €*

5 La Fougére
This multi-award winning restaurant is set on a hill a short walk from the town centre. It offers stunning views of the water alongside the delicious fare. ✎ *Knockranny House Hotel, Westport, Co Mayo • Map M2 • 098 28600 • €€€€*

6 Hungry Monk Café
Enjoy a lunch or gourmet snack at this down-to-earth village café. The home-made baking and deserts alone are worth stopping for. ✎ *Abbey St, Cong, Co. Mayo • Map M2 • 094 9545842 • €*

7 Kylemore Abbey
Irish stew and beef and Guinness casserole with ingredients from the Abbey's garden are some of the traditional dishes on offer. ✎ *Kylemore Abbey, Connemara, Co. Galway • Map N3 • 095 52001 • €*

8 Newport House
This restaurant in a lovely Georgian mansion bases its menu on fresh produce from its own farm, gardens and fishery, and smokes its own salmon. Also has a superb wine cellar. ✎ *Newport • Map M2 • 098 41222 • Dis. access • €€€*

9 Rosleague Manor
Connemara lamb and local seafood are specialities of the house, served with the best local ingredients. ✎ *Letterfrack • Map M2 • 095 41101 • Open to non-residents by reservation • €€*

10 Crockets on the Quay
Affordable, friendly and relaxed restaurant and bar on the quay, beside the River Moy. Choose from bar meals (great chowder) or a full menu featuring modern Irish cuisine. ✎ *Ballina • Map L2 • 096 75930 • Dis. access • €€*

 Note: *Unless otherwise stated, all restaurants accept credit cards and serve vegetarian meals*

Left **Lough Swilly, Inishowen Peninsula** Right **Hargadon's Pub, Sligo**

Yeats Country and the Northwest

THE NORTHWEST OF IRELAND IS AMONG THE LEAST EXPLORED *areas of the country, and yet it incorporates some of the finest and most dramatic scenery, with its beautiful, wide sandy beaches, towering mountains, woodland and forest parks. Driving is really the best way to tour this part of the country as public transport is all but non-existent, and it gives the visitor the freedom to explore at whim. The region's colloquial name is in honour of the two great Irish brothers, Jack B and WB Yeats, artist and poet respectively, who hailed from the ancient Celtic town of Sligo. This was also the legendary power base of the warrior Queen Maeve of Connaught and is packed with prehistoric sites. Donegal has played a more historic role throughout the centuries but was finally left isolated when it was excluded from the new Northern Ireland in 1921. Its abandonment has left it with little in common with its fellow counties, historically or geographically.*

WB Yeats statue, Sligo

 Sights

1. Inishowen Peninsula
2. Glenveagh National Park
3. Sligo
4. Horn Head
5. Lissadell & Drumcliffe
6. Lough Key & Boyle
7. Parke's Castle
8. Donegal
9. Killybegs
10. Letterkenny

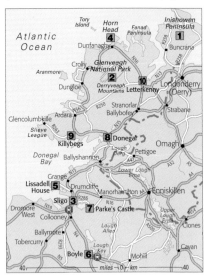

Inishowen Peninsula

Undiscovered by so many, this glorious corner in the far northwest has possibly the finest scenery in Ireland, with the spectacular Slieve Snaght Mountain in the centre, Foyle and Swilly lakes to east and west, and the dune-fringed beaches facing the Atlantic. The peninsula also has its share of drama headlands and boasts most northwes Malin Hea

quirky, arty shops, good book-shops and fine restaurants. To the east of town is the lovely Lough Gill, with a number of woodland walks. The brooding outline of Benbulben Mountain and the beaches of Strandhill and Rosses Point are only

…sula …natic …sts Ireland's …terly point at …d. 🕭 *Co Donegal • Map K4*

Glenveagh National Park
The extraordinary quartzite cone of Mount Errigal dominates the Derryveagh mountain range in this wild part of Donegal. It overlooks the Glenveagh National Park, which incorporates the beautiful Lough Veagh Valley, and Poison Glen. One theory behind the name is that British soldiers were fed Irish spurge, a poisonous plant indigenous to the area, to murder them. 🕭 *Co Donegal • 076 1002537 • Map K4 • Open Mar–Oct: 9am–6pm daily; Nov–Feb: 9am–5pm daily • Dis. access • Free*

Sligo
This busy market town is home to the excellent Model Arts Centre and Niland Gallery, which has a collection of Jack B Yeats's paintings, as well as

…lly …minutes …ve away. 🕭 *Co Sligo • Map L3*

Horn Head
This dramatic 180-m (600-ft) rockface is home to hundreds of seabirds, including guillemots, gulls and puffins, which swoop in and out of the crevices hewn into the rock. The headland is covered in purple heather and the views over the Atlantic are stupendous. 🕭 *Co Donegal • Map K4*

Lissadell and Drumcliffe
Just north of Sligo is Drumcliffe church, where WB Yeats *(see p34)* is buried, and the visitors' centre focuses on items and books relating to the poet. The area was a great inspiration to Yeats and he was a frequent visitor at the rather forbidding Lissadell House a few miles to the west. Lissadell was home to the Gore-Booth family, who were active in the fight for Irish freedom. 🕭 *Ballinfull, Co Sligo • Map L3 • Lissadell House: closed to the public*

Lissadell House

Following pages: **Milk churns, rural Ireland**

The Gaeltachts

The area around Donegal is one of the largest Gaelic-speaking *(Gaeltacht)* regions of the country. Until the 17th century most of the Irish population spoke Gaelic, the only other language being Latin. During British rule, use of the language diminished as English took over. However, in *Gaeltacht* areas, Irish speakers cling fiercely to their native culture.

St Eunan's Cathedral, Letterkenny

Lough Key and Boyle

One of the best spots for viewing this magnificent lake is from the main Sligo-to-Boyle road. The Lough Key Forest Park has numerous walks along the lakeside and through the woods. Boyle is an appealing nearby town with a ruined abbey, interesting museum and some fine Georgian architecture. ✆ *Co Roscommon • Map M3*

Parke's Castle

Built by a Captain Robert Parke in 1609, and overlooking Lough Gill, this fortified manor house was erected on the site of an earlier tower house. The foundations and moat of this earlier structure are incorporated into the castle but otherwise it is a fine example of a plantation house. You can visit the castle by road or by boat on the Lough Gill cruise. ✆ *Fivemile Bourne, Co Leitrim • 071 916 4149 • Map L3 • Open Apr–Sep: 10am–6pm daily; last adm 5pm • Adm*

Parke's Castle

Donegal

Donegal is most famous for its tweed production *(see p125)* with Magee's the biggest manu-facturer based here. The Diamond, a triangular central market, is at the heart of the town and an obelisk in the centre commemorates four Franciscans who wrote *Annals of the Four Masters* in the 1630s. This extraordinary opus follows the history of the Gaelic people from the Great Flood up to the 17th century. ✆ *Co Donegal • Map L4*

Killybegs

An exciting place to be when the boats come in, Killy-begs is one of the busiest fishing ports in the country. As the trawlers unload their catches gulls squawk over the water in an attempt to claim a discarded morsel. ✆ *Co Donegal • Map L3*

Letterkenny

Donegal's largest town is flanked by the Derryveagh Mountains to the west and the Sperrin Mountains to the east. Its main street, said to be the longest in Ireland, is overlooked by the Gothic St Eunan's Cathedral. The County Museum has a good display on local history. ✆ *Co Donegal • Map K4*

Price Categories

For a three-course meal for one with half a bottle of wine (or equivalent meal), taxes and extra charges.

€ under €35
€€ €35–€45
€€€ €45–€65
€€€€ €65–€90
€€€€€ over €90

Above **The Mill Restaurant**

🔟 Places to Eat and Drink

1 Cromleach Lodge
Signposted from the N4 at Castlebaldwin, this restaurant and country house has beautiful views of Lough Arrow mountains. Eating here is a gourmet experience with simple dishes expertly prepared.
🖎 *Lough Arrow, Castlebaldwin, Co Sligo • Map M3 • 071 916 5155 • Closed lunch • Dis. access • €€*

2 Rathmullan House
A grand country house hotel, described as an institution in Donegal. Gourmet dinners are made using ingredients from their walled garden and served in the Pavilion room. 🖎 *Rathmullan, Co Donegal • Map L3 • 074 915 8188 • Dis. access • €€€*

3 Woodhill House
This coastal manor house has an excellent French-style restaurant. Try the fresh seafood landed at the nearby fishing village of Killybegs. 🖎 *Ardara, Co Donegal • Map L3 • 074 954 1112 • €€€*

4 Coach Lane Restaurant
A delicious variety of cooking styles and dishes, such as Clew Bay scallops, free range poussin and local Lissadell mussels and clams. 🖎 *1–2 Lord Edward St, Sligo • Map L3 • 071 916 2417 • €€€*

5 Yeats Tavern
This large, bustling tavern is a popular stopping place on the way to Donegal. Generous helpings and a huge choice. 🖎 *Drumcliffe, Co Sligo • Map L3 • 071 916 3117 • €€*

6 Montmartre
The creative menus at this stylish restaurant feature authentic French and European cuisine. Magnificent wine list.
🖎 *1 Market Yard, Sligo, Co Sligo • Map L3 • 071 916 9901 • Dis. access • €€€*

7 Kealy's Seafood Bar
Beside the pier, this atmospheric restaurant-bar serves first-class seafood and a range of meat and vegetarian dishes. Traditional music most Sundays.
🖎 *Greencastle, Co Donegal • Map K5 • 074 938 1010 • Dis. access • €€*

8 Fiddlers Creek
A popular pub and restaurant on the Garavogue River serving tasty sizzling seafood, meat and poultry dishes. Dine in the Western-themed restaurant or the cosy bar. 🖎 *Rockwood Parade, Sligo, Co Sligo • Map L3 • 071 914 1866 • Dis. access • €€*

9 The Mill Restaurant
An old flax mill converted into a family-run restaurant which offers tasy roasts and seafood dishes. Also a small guesthouse.
🖎 *Dunfanaghy, Co Donegal • Map K4 • 074 913 6985 • Dis. access • €€€*

10 Smuggler's Creek Inn
Take a table with a view in this family-run restaurant overlooking the sweep of Donegal Bay. The speciality is seafood but they also provide a good range of other dishes. 🖎 *Rossnowlagh, Co Donegal • Map L3 • 071 985 2366 • €€*

Left **Mount Stewart House** Right **Derry**

Northern Ireland

NORTHERN IRELAND REMAINED UNDER UK *administration when the rest of Ireland became independent in 1921 and blends the two nations of which it is a part. A distinctive society has developed here, especially the historic cultural divide between Nationalists (Catholics of Irish descent) and Loyalists (Protestants of English and Scottish descent) – each group has its own traditions. Yet between Northern Ireland and the Republic there are more similarities than differences, from music, to food and drink, to the landscape – indeed, some of the north's scenery is among the best in the country.*

Ulster-American Folk Park

Sights

1 Castle Coole
2 Giant's Causeway
3 Mount Stewart House
4 Glens of Antrim
5 Lower Loch Erne
6 Armagh
7 Belfast
8 Ulster-American Folk Park
9 Florence Court
10 Derry

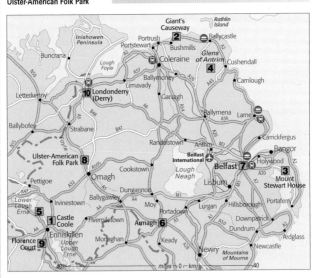

Castle Coole

The mansion built in the 1790s for the Earl of Belmore by James Wyatt stands grandly at the end of a long driveway and is set in impressive grounds. The house has been almost completely rebuilt in its original Neo-Classical style as commissioned by the first earl, while the sumptuous interior is richly decorated with elaborate plasterwork. The lavish 18th- and 19th-century Regency furnishings are those favoured by the second earl during the 1820s.

 Enniskilxlen • 028 6632 2690 • Map L4 • House: Open 11am–5pm Sat & Sun; Grounds: 10am–7pm Sat & Sun • Adm

Giant's Causeway

The Causeway, a designated a World Heritage Site since 1986, is a truly remarkable natural spectacle, its thousands of extraordinary hexagonal pillars of basalt rock clustered like a gigantic piece of honeycomb. The rocks descend from seafront cliffs into the water and disappear from view. Supposedly created by legendary warrior Fionn mac Cumhaill as his stepping stones to Scotland *(see p38)*, Giant's Causeway was really created by a volcanic eruption 60 million years ago. There's an informative visitors' centre nearby.

 Bushmills, Co Antrim, 028 2073 1855 • Map K5

Giant's Causeway

Mount Stewart House

The grandly aristocratic 18th-century home of the Marquess of Londonderry displays a superb art collection, and stands in wonderful landscaped gardens with remarkable plant collections. There is some extraordinary topiary, exquisite planned views and numerous odd stonecarvings representing creatures such as dodos and dinosaurs. Also in the grounds is the elegant octagonal Temple of the Winds, a copy of a Classical relic near Athens. *Strangford Lough, near Newtownards • 028 4278 8387 • Map L6 • Lakeside Gardens: Open 10am–5pm daily; House & Formal Gardens: mid-Mar–Oct: 11am–5pm daily • Adm*

Glens of Antrim

Among the finest scenery in Ireland is the coast of County Antrim, where nine beautiful valleys (glens) cut deeply through high rolling hills to descend grandly into the sea. The effect, seen from the shore road, is spectacular. Follow the A2 through Carnlough, with its tiny harbour, through Waterfoot, with waterfalls and a Forest Park, all the way up to the Giant's Causeway. *Map K5*

Lower Loch Erne

The serene waters and small islands extending north from Enniskillen can be explored by boat, or encircled by road. Devenish Island, reached from the east bank, is the remarkable site of 6th-century monastic ruins, a Celtic High Cross, and an 30-m (100-ft) Round Tower. Boa Island, reached by a causeway, is noted for a strange double-faced Celtic stone carving. Another group of curious stone figures stands on White Island. *Map L4*

Armagh

Armagh

The city where Queen Macha built her fortress some 3,000 years ago, Armagh has a curious role in Ulster's religious divide. St Patrick based himself here, and the city is considered the ecclesiastical capital of both communities, with a Catholic and a Protestant cathedral, each dedicated to Patrick. The town also has a good museum and astronomy centre. ® *Map L5*

Belfast

Northern Ireland's capital is a vibrant Victorian city with shops, pubs, museums and galleries. Call at the Belfast Welcome Centre for details of the attractions in and around the city. ® *Map L6 • Belfast Welcome Centre: 9 Donegall Sq N; Open daily.*

Ulster-American Folk Park

Many Americans can trace their roots back to 19th-century rural Ulster, and many, like local-born millionaire Thomas Mellon, did very well in their new home. The Folk Park, built around Mellon's birthplace, reconstructs their lives on both sides of the Atlantic. The open-air museum contains more than 30 historic buildings, settler homesteads, churches and an emigrant ship. ® *Near Omagh • Map L4 • Open Mar–Sep: 10am–5pm Tue–Sun; Oct–Feb: 10am–4pm Tue–Fri, 11am–4pm Sat & Sun • Adm*

Florence Court

The grandiose 18th-century Palladian mansion originally belonged to the Earls of Enniskillen. Among the original features are an icehouse and a water-driven sawmill. The interior is decorated with ornamental plasterwork and period furnishings. ® *A32, near Enniskillen • Map L4 • Opening hours vary – refer to the website (www.nationaltrust.org) for more information*

Derry

At the heart of Derry (Londonderry) is a fascinating walled Plantation town, its 400-year-old fortifications almost intact. Free Derry Corner contains the famous political mural "You Are Now Entering Free Derry", painted in 1969. ® *Map K4*

City Hall, Belfast

Above **Crown Liquor Saloon**

Price Categories

For a three-course meal for one with half a bottle of wine (or equivalent meal), taxes and extra charges.

£	under £25
££	£25–£35
£££	£35–£55
££££	£55–£70
£££££	over £70

🔟 Places to Eat

1 Deane's Restaurant
This pleasant French brasserie-style restaurant offers impressively elegant dining. The decor is minimalist but the food itself is often exciting and innovative. ◈ 28–40 Howard St, Belfast • Map L6 • 028 9033 1134 • Dis. access • £££

2 OX
Offering a menu that is centred around local and seasonal produce, this award-winning eatery overlooking the Lagan serves dishes like hay-baked beetroot and Skeaghanore duck. ◈ 1 Oxford St, Belfast • Map L6 • 028 9031 4121 • Dis. access • ££

3 The Morning Star
This historic 19th-century pub-restaurant features fine local seafood, meat and poultry including home-made sausages. ◈ 17–19 Pottinger's Entry, Belfast • Map L6 • 028 9023 5986 • ££

4 Crown Liquor Saloon
Local favourites are served at this lovely old pub, such as cottage pie for two, and venison and red wine sausages. ◈ 46 Great Victoria St, Belfast • Map L6 • 028 9024 3187 • £

5 Pier 36
This award-winning pub serves great seafood and local game, and bakes its own bread on a range right in the middle of the dining area. ◈ The Parade, Donaghadee • Map K6 • 028 9188 4466 • Dis. access • ££

6 James Street South Bar and Grill
Renowned for its beef, which is cooked over a charcoal grill, this restaurant has a cool contemporary vibe, and a fantastic drinks menu. ◈ 21 James Street South, Belfast • Map L6 • 028 9560 0700 • ££

7 The Portaferry Hotel
This restaurant on the shores of Strangford Lough has a high reputation for top-quality shellfish and other seafood, most of it from the waters of the lake. ◈ The Strand, Portaferry • Map L6 • 028 4272 8231 • Dis. access • ££

8 Bushmills Inn
In the village that produces Ulster's finest whiskey is an atmospheric re-creation of an old coaching inn, with open fires and gas lighting. The menu ranges from local beef to fresh salmon. ◈ 9 Dunluce Rd • Map K5 • 028 2073 3000 • Dis. access • ££

9 Uno Restaurant
A popular bistro-style restaurant and wine bar. Dishes range from comforting macaroni to steak with brandy cream. ◈ 17 Belmore St, Enniskillen • Map L4 • 028 6634 2622 • Dis. access • £

10 Mourne Seafood Bar
Sea-fresh local seafood, including shellfish from the bar's own beds. Local steak and chicken are also on the menu. ◈ 10 Main St, Dundrum, Newcastle • Map U4 • 028 437 51377 • ££

> Note that, unlike the rest of Ireland, the currency in Northern Ireland has not changed to the euro but remains pounds sterling.

Left **Lough Swilly, Inishowen Peninsula** Right **Hargadon's Pub, Sligo**

Yeats Country and the Northwest

THE NORTHWEST OF IRELAND IS AMONG THE LEAST EXPLORED *areas of the country, and yet it incorporates some of the finest and most dramatic scenery, with its beautiful, wide sandy beaches, towering mountains, woodland and forest parks. Driving is really the best way to tour this part of the country as public transport is all but non-existent, and it gives the visitor the freedom to explore at whim. The region's colloquial name is in honour of the two great Irish brothers, Jack B and WB Yeats, artist and poet respectively, who hailed from the ancient Celtic town of Sligo. This was also*

the legendary power base of the warrior Queen Maeve of Connaught and is packed with prehistoric sites. Donegal has played a more historic role throughout the centuries but was finally left isolated when it was excluded from the new Northern Ireland in 1921. Its abandonment has left it with little in common with its fellow counties, historically or geographically.

WB Yeats statue, Sligo

🔟 Sights

1. Inishowen Peninsula
2. Glenveagh National Park
3. Sligo
4. Horn Head
5. Lissadell & Drumcliffe
6. Lough Key & Boyle
7. Parke's Castle
8. Donegal
9. Killybegs
10. Letterkenny

Price Categories

For a three-course meal for one with half a bottle of wine (or equivalent meal), taxes and extra charges.	€ under €35
	€€ €35–€45
	€€€ €45–€65
	€€€€ €65–€90
	€€€€€ over €90

Above **Renvyle House**

🔟 Places to Eat

1 Mitchell's
A family-style restaurant in the Connemara village of Clifden, serving comforting, home-style food, such as seafood and poultry dishes, in a relaxed setting. ⊗ *Market St, Clifden, Co. Galway • Map M1 • 095 21867 • €€*

2 Burke's Bar & Restaurant
This lively pub in the village of Clonbur serves meat, fish and poultry dishes as well as home-baked scones and soda bread. Outside dining in summer. ⊗ *Mount Gable House, Clonbur, Co. Galway • Map N3 • 094 9546175 • Dis. access • €€*

3 Renvyle House
A gracious country house-style hotel on the shores of the Atlantic serving superb seafood, Connemara lamb, and a range of other classic Irish and European dishes. Booking is advisable. ⊗ *Renvyle • Map M1 • 095 46100 • Dis. access • €€€*

4 JW Brasserie
Award-winning contemporary Irish restaurant, popular with locals and tourists alike. ⊗ *The Octagon, Westport, Co. Mayo • Map M2 • 098 25027 • Dis. access • €*

5 La Fougére
This multi-award winning restaurant is set on a hill a short walk from the town centre. It offers stunning views of the water alongside the delicious fare. ⊗ *Knockranny House Hotel, Westport, Co Mayo • Map M2 • 098 28600 • €€€€*

6 Hungry Monk Café
Enjoy a lunch or gourmet snack at this down-to-earth village café. The home-made baking and deserts alone are worth stopping for. ⊗ *Abbey St, Cong, Co. Mayo • Map M2 • 094 9545842 • €*

7 Kylemore Abbey
Irish stew and beef and Guinness casserole with ingredients from the Abbey's garden are some of the traditional dishes on offer. ⊗ *Kylemore Abbey, Connemara, Co. Galway • Map N3 • 095 52001 • €*

8 Newport House
This restaurant in a lovely Georgian mansion bases its menu on fresh produce from its own farm, gardens and fishery, and smokes its own salmon. Also has a superb wine cellar. ⊗ *Newport • Map M2 • 098 41222 • Dis. access • €€€*

9 Rosleague Manor
Connemara lamb and local seafood are specialities of the house, served with the best local ingredients. ⊗ *Letterfrack • Map M2 • 095 41101 • Open to non-residents by reservation • €€*

10 Crockets on the Quay
Affordable, friendly and relaxed restaurant and bar on the quay, beside the River Moy. Choose from bar meals (great chowder) or a full menu featuring modern Irish cuisine. ⊗ *Ballina • Map L2 • 096 75930 • Dis. access • €€*

 Note: *Unless otherwise stated, all restaurants accept credit cards and serve vegetarian meals*

Left **Dublin Bus** Centre **Parking sign** Right **DART electric train**

TOP 10 Getting Around Dublin

City Buses
Dublin Bus runs a comprehensive network around the city, every 10–20 minutes from 6am to 11:30pm. All buses operate an autofare system so make sure you have change or a travel pass. One-day, three-day, five-day, weekly and monthly travel passes are available from tourist centres and most newsagents. Nitelink Buses operate every 30 minutes from midnight to 4am Friday and Saturday from Westmoreland Street, D'Olier Street, College Green, St Stephen's Green and O'Connell Street. Travel passes are not valid on these buses, which have a flat charge of €6 – €5 with a Leap card. Green and cream bus stops are for the Hop-on-Hop-off tourist buses and are situated at 16 major tourist points around the city. ✆ *Dublin Bus: 01-873 4222, www.dublinbus.ie*

DART
DART (Dublin Area Rapid Transport) is an electric train service covering 28 stations from picturesque Malahide and Howth to the north of the city to Greystones in County Wicklow, with a few city centre stops. The last train leaves the city centre at 11:30pm. ✆ *DART: 1850 366 222, www.irishrail.ie*

Luas
This light railway system has eased city centre traffic in Dublin. It is made up of two non-connecting lines. The Green Line operates between St Stephen's Green and Sandyford and then on to Cherrywood. The Red Line runs from the O2 Arena, past Connolly station to Tallaght and Saggart. ✆ *Luas: www.luas.ie*

Walking
The centre of Dublin is compact and very easy to walk around, and increasing numbers of streets are being pedestrianized.

Taxis
Taxi ranks can be found at the airport, main stations, large hotels and many designated areas around the city. They can also be hailed in the street. Fares are metered, with the base rate around €4. There is also the "taxi app", Hailo, which allows you to order a taxi, track its arrival, and pay by debit or credit card. ✆ *National Radio Cabs: 01-677 2222*

Rental Cars
All the main car rental companies have desks at the airport and in the city. A full driving licence is required and age restriction is generally between 23 and 70 years. Rental usually includes unlimited mileage and third party fire and theft insurance. ✆ *Europcar: 1800 948 855, www.europcar.ie*

Road Rules
City and town speed limits are 30 kmph, outskirts are 80 kmph, with 100 kmph on open roads and 120 kmph on motorways. Speed cameras are in frequent use and on-the-spot fines can be issued by the police. Road signs come in both English and Irish and kilometres.

Petrol Stations
Most rental cars take unleaded fuel, but leaded and diesel are also available. The nearest petrol stations to the centre are at Ballsbridge, Donnybrook and Usher's Quay.

Parking
There is plenty of parking available in the centre, with electronic signs at various strategic points giving up-to-the-minute availability of spaces. Clamping is in operation throughout Dublin for illegal parking.

Trains
Ireland's train service is operated by Irish Rail (Iarnród Éireann), with trains to most cities and main towns. Direct services are efficient but some areas such as Donegal *(see p112)* are not served by the railway and there are no coastal routes in the south, east or north, so these areas must be explored by car or bus. ✆ *Irish Rail: 1850 366 222, www.irishrail.ie*

Left **Irish Tourist Board logo** Centre **Irish-English sign** Right **Driving in Dublin**

Sources of Information

Tourist Offices

Discover Ireland has a number of information and booking offices around the country as well as offices in the capital in Suffolk St, O'Connell St, the Arrivals Hall at Dublin Airport and the Ferry Terminal in Dun Laoghaire.
🌐 www.visitdublin.com, www.discoverireland.ie

Discounts and Concessions

There are reductions on entrance tickets to many historic sites and attractions, on some transport, and even on some travel packages, for students, children, the unemployed, senior citizens and families. Carry photo ID. To visit several sights at a discount, buy a Heritage Card (see p124).

Business Hours

Most shops and businesses are open 9am to 6pm, Monday to Friday. Banks open Monday to Friday 10am to 4pm (sometimes until 5pm on Thursday); post offices Monday to Friday 9am to 5:30pm, Saturday 9am to 12:30pm. Pubs open Monday to Thursday 10:30am to 11:30pm, Friday to Saturday 10:30am to 12:30am, Sunday 12:30pm to 11pm.

Internet

Internet cafés can be found in most towns, and throughout Dublin. Charges are generally around €1 for 15 minutes. Public libraries also offer free Internet access, while free Wi-Fi is common in Dublin cafés and bars.

Driving

Ireland has one of the highest percentages of driving fatalities in Europe. Drink-driving is a problem and speed limits are often ignored, though a "penalty points" system is improving the situation. Congestion in towns is high, but rural roads are relatively traffic-free. Even main roads may have only two lanes – pull onto the hard-shoulder to let others overtake. Speed limits are 120 kmph (74 mph) on motorways, 80–100 kmph (49–62 mph) on main roads, 50 kmph (31 mph) in towns. Drive on the left. Yellow lines indicate parking restrictions. All types of fuel are available.

Road Signs

Ireland uses Europe's international pictorial system of road signs. Confusing signs that give two alternative routes to the same place without stating the distances are commonplace in rural Ireland. When given, distances may be approximate. Officially, the Republic uses kilometres (green signs), but many roadsigns are in miles (white signs). Often, place names are given in Irish and English.

Climate

The weather in Ireland is wet and mild all year round, but generally without extremes. It rarely freezes except on uplands, while summer can see some hot spells.

Embassies and Consulates

Britain and the US both have embassies in Dublin (see box). Most other countries have an embassy or consulate in the city – consult the Golden Pages telephone book.

Tipping

Service charges of 10–15 per cent may be added to bills in hotels and restaurants. Tip porters 50 cents or €1. Bar staff and taxi drivers need not be tipped.

Northern Ireland

The border crossing between the Republic and Northern Ireland is normally simple, with few formalities. However, check with car rental companies that you may take the vehicle across the border, which is still a national frontier.

Embassies

British Embassy
29 Merrion Rd, Ballsbridge • Bus Nos. 7, 8 • 01-205 3700

US Embassy
42 Elgin Rd, Ballsbridge • Bus Nos. 7, 8 • 01-668 8777

Opening times of museums and other sights vary and are given next to their appropriate entries in this guide.

Left **Rush-hour traffic** Right **Boarding an Irish bus**

🔟 Things to Avoid

1 Drink-driving
There are very strict drink-driving laws in Ireland and you can be stopped and breathalysed at any time. Within the city, most places can be reached on foot, and restaurants are very happy to call cabs.

2 Unsafe Areas
It is unwise to wander around any badly lit areas of any city at night, and Dublin is no exception. It is also advisable not to walk around on your own late at night. There are areas of the city that have a reputation for being more dangerous than others – parts of the Northside are a bit rough after dark, so stick to the main thoroughfares such as O'Connell Street (see p61). On the Southside, around Dolphin's Barn, beyond Portobello, is a notorious area for drug-related crime, so avoid that both day and night, and similarly Summerhill off Gardiner Street on the Northside. However neither of these areas has anything to draw the tourist so you are unlikely to find yourself there unless lost.

3 Carrying Valuables
It is always a mistake to carry valuables around with you when you're sightseeing, so leave them in the hotel safe. If you're driving, never leave anything visible in the car to tempt a break-in. Like any capital city, beware of pickpockets. Don't put temptation in their way by leaving bags open and valuables visible.

4 Rush Hour Traffic
The traffic has got much worse in Dublin over the last few years and the rush hour lasts from about 8–9:30am and 5–7pm so allow extra time if you need to travel between these times. Traffic problems on the route to the airport have been improved somewhat by the opening of the Port Tunnel.

5 Smoking
Smoking in the workplace is banned in the Republic and Northern Ireland. Pubs, nightclubs, restaurants and cafés are also all smoke free, although many pubs and clubs have outdoor smoking areas.

6 Drinking in Hotels
It is best to avoid drinking in hotel bars unless money is no object. Prices are always higher than in local bars and pubs, and a gratuity may be added.

7 Taxis
Deregulation of taxis has meant that there is now a surplus of cabs. At the weekend, the cautious may prefer to book ahead, but by and large it's easy to hail one along any main road. If you are at a restaurant, you could ask your waiter to call you a taxi.

8 Parking Fines
Dublin's traffic wardens are very sharp and quite thick on the ground, so make sure you don't overrun your time as you'll be fined immediately. Clampers are also about all over the city, and it is time-consuming and expensive to get released.

9 International Rugby Weekends
From February to April the Six Nations Cup is played out between Italy, Wales, Scotland, Ireland, France and England with matches in the various countries. These weekends are great "craic" especially if the Irish win, but it is worth noting that hotel prices increase and the city is overcrowded.

10 Countrywide Public Transport
The public transport system outside of Dublin is generally poor (see p121). There is a rail service to the main cities from Dublin but it is difficult to tour from one place to another as rail and bus links are limited. If you need to use public transport make sure you have researched your route beforehand.

Left **Heritage Card** Right **Bicycles in Dublin**

TOP 10 Dublin on a Budget

1 Sightseeing for Free

Most of the properties owned and run by the Office of Public Works (OPW), the State Heritage Service, are reasonably priced, while all national museums, galleries and libraries are free. There is a minimal charge for entry to some city churches but around the country they are generally free.

2 Sightseeing at a Discount

Sights and museums are either privately or state-run so discounts vary from site to site. On average, the concessions given for children, over 60s and students work out at about one third of the price of the full adult ticket. If you are planning to visit a number of sights consider the Dublin Pass. It gives free entry to more than 33 attractions, a skip-the-queue facility and discounts in certain shops and restaurants. It is available for periods of 1, 2, 3, and 6 days online or from a tourist office (see p122). The Heritage Card and National Trust cards for NI offer entry discounts for one year. ⊗ Dublin Pass: www. dublinpass.ie • Heritage Card: www.heritageireland. ie • National Trust: www. nationaltrust.org.uk

3 Discount Travel Cards

Youth and student discounts are available on presentation of an International Student ID Card (ISIC) for some museums, and rail and bus travel. Train discount cards include Irish Rail's Trekker Four Day card, but you need to be covering quite a distance to make it worthwhile. The most useful in Ireland is the combined bus and rail pass, the Irish Explorer Ticket. It covers all Intercity train and bus lines and the DART in Dublin (see p121).

4 Cheap Eateries

There is no shortage of these in the city, including McDonald's and Burger King, Beshoffs for fish and chips and a limitless supply of cafés and juice bars. Most small towns have a take-away of some description and garages and Spar shops throughout the country usually have a hot food counter.

5 Bicycle Rental

This is a cheap and fast way of getting about, and Dublin Bikes provides the capital with a bike-share rental scheme akin to those run in cities such as Paris, Brussels and Vienna. Bikes can be picked up from 71 stations across the city. The system is designed for short-term rental, but you will need a credit card to register at one of the bike stations. ⊗ www.dublinbikes.ie

6 Cross-Country Buses

Ireland's public transport network is not brilliant (see p121). Trains link the main towns and cities but getting from one regional town to another is not easy. On intercity routes it is much cheaper to go by bus.

7 Hostel Accommodation

There are numerous hostels around the country. Many of the Dublin ones are of a good quality and you can get single and even double rooms at very low prices.

8 Big Breakfasts

The full Irish breakfast in hotels is a huge affair and will set you up for the day.

9 Off-season Travel

Travelling out of season and avoiding special weekends will save you money. Prices are hiked up during Rugby International weekends (see p123), St Patrick's weekend (see p41) and bank holidays. In winter there are excellent hotel deals.

10 Shopping Carefully

Many items are no cheaper in Ireland than elsewhere, including tweeds. Seek out markets and craft shops where you could pick up original items for much less than in stores.

  Another option for cheap accommodation in Ireland is the universities during student holiday times.

Left **Celtic Claddagh ring** Centre **Aran jersey** Right **Enamel brooch**

10 Things to Buy

Linen
Ireland is world famous for its linen and there are some beautiful, original designs to be found. There is usually a selection on offer in most tourist shops. The choice includes embroidered bedcovers and table-cloths, linen pillowcases and duvet covers. At the less grand end of the scale, small embroidered handkerchiefs make good gifts and tea towels can be found everywhere.

Woollen Jerseys
Ireland is justly renowned for its terrific jerseys, and the Aran is the most famous. It can be fun to buy them in the west of Ireland if you're travelling around, although the range is probably better in Dublin. The larger department stores, specialist jersey outlets and tourist shops are the best places to try.

Ceramics
There are a number of excellent contemporary pottery companies available in most of the larger department stores such as Kilkenny Shop or Arnotts. But search out craft shops around the country for original pieces by individuals like Louis Mulcahy.

Tweed
One of the most famous tweed-producing areas is Donegal (see p112) where tweed can be bought either ready-made as clothing or off the bale as lengths of cloth. Hats and waist-coats are popular and come in a variety of tweeds. Most smaller items are widely available in tourist shops, but for the full tweed suit you'd be better off with the specialist. Try Kevin and Howlin (see p57).

Jewellery
You can find Celtic jewellery in some form or another all over the city, but be careful of the quality. For the best in contemporary hand-crafted jewellery, go to Designyard on Nassau Street (see p57). This will give you an idea of top quality and prices. If you're feeling adventurous you can commission a piece. There is a huge variety on offer all over the country, from ancient Celtic to modern designs.

Musical Instruments
The tin whistle is one of the most commonly found traditional Irish musical instruments and cheap replicas can be found all over the city. Enquire in a proper music shop if you are looking for a decent one. The *bodhrán* is a goatskin handheld drum; this too is widely reproduced but the good ones need to be specially sought out. Visit master *bodhrán* maker Malachy Kearns in Roundstone, Galway. Handmade harps are also a particular speciality in Dublin and Mayo.

Smoked Salmon
Irish smoked salmon is world famous and is widely exported. Wrights of Howth (see p75) has outlets at the airport and at Howth, but most fishmongers stock wild salmon.

Whiskey
Jamesons (see p63) is probably the best known Irish brand and is a fine smooth blend; Bushmills is also a popular whiskey produced in the north. For everyday whiskey drinking the average Irish person would probably settle for Powers – an altogether rougher experience.

Crystal and Glassware
Waterford Crystal is the best known producer of glassware in Ireland (see p83) but other quality producers exist. Galway Irish Crystal and Tipperary Crystal are two contenders, with Louise Kennedy Crystal tending towards contemporary design.

Chocolates and Cheese
The Irish are very good at producing chocolates and a leading brand name is Butlers. Ireland is also famous for its cheeses. Cashel Blue, Durrus and Cooleeney are only a few of a large number worth sampling.

Left **Irish post sign** Right **Irish national daily newspapers**

🔟 Banking and Communications

1 Banks

Allied Irish Bank (AIB), the Bank of Ireland, the Ulster Bank, the KBC bank, and the Permanent-TSB are the five retail banks in the Republic. They are mostly open Monday to Friday, 10am to 4pm. ATMs (cashpoints) are located outside most banks in the city, and are the fastest and cheapest way to get local currency, drawing money directly from your account if you belong to a co-operating bank. All UK cashcards can be used at these machines.

2 Currency

Ireland joined the European Monetary Union in 1999, with 11 other EU countries, and the euro has been the sole legal tender since early 2002. Coin denominations are 1, 2, 5, 10, 20 and 50 cents, and €1 and €2, while notes come in denominations of €5, €10, €20, €50, €100, €200 and €500. There are 100 cents to €1.

3 Credit Cards and Travellers' Cheques

Visa and MasterCard are the most widely accepted cards; American Express and Diners Club less so. You can withdraw cash from ATMs using credit cards. The rise of ATMs is fast supplanting the need for traveller's cheques. Debit cards, such as Visa debit, are widely accepted.

4 Exchanging Money

For all foreign currencies outside of the EMU, the banks offer the best rates of exchange. Bureaux de change rates vary but they are likely to be better than hotel rates if the banks are closed. Some department stores offer exchange facilities.

5 Post

Most post offices open from 9am to 5:30pm Monday to Friday and 9am to 1pm on Saturdays. The General Post Office in O'Connell Street *(see p62)* is open all day, seven days a week. Stamps can also be purchased from some newsagents and shops. Post boxes in Ireland are green. The easiest way to receive mail in Dublin is to have it sent to your hotel but a *poste restante* service is also available from major post offices.

6 Telephones

The majority of phone booths are controlled by Eircom. Public pay-phones are on the decrease. The wording around the top of each booth indicates whether it takes coins, phone-cards or credit cards – most in Dublin are now card-operated. The cheapest time to make calls is after 6pm and at weekends. Calls made from hotels can be expensive.

7 Phonecards

Pre-paid phonecards, available in several denominations, are useful for long distance calls. These, as well as card-credits for mobile phones, can be bought at newsagents, post offices, supermarkets and other retail outlets.

8 Internet

You can find an Internet café in most areas of Dublin and most hotels also offer Internet facilities. Failing that, try the nearest public library or post office.

9 Newspapers

The Republic of Ireland has eight national daily papers and six Sunday papers. Quality dailies include the *Irish Times*, the *Irish Independent* and the *Irish Examiner*. Ireland's daily tabloids include the *Irish Mirror* and the *Star*. Dublin's evening paper is the *Herald*. All British papers are on sale throughout Dublin and larger newsagents stock international newspapers.

10 Radio and Television

Ireland has five national television channels: RTE 1, RTE 2, TV3, 3E and TG4. There are six national radio stations including an Irish langu-age service, and many local ones. The five British channels can be picked up through cable and satellite connections.

Left **Pharmacy sign** Centre **Police station sign** Right **Police car**

🔟 Security and Health

1 Emergency numbers

Dial 999 or 112 in an emergency and you will be connected to the service you require – police, fire, ambulance or coastguard.

2 Police

The police force in the Irish Republic is called the *Garda Siochana*. It was established in 1922, and its headquarters are in Phoenix Park.

3 Hospitals

Beaumont, St James's and St Vincent's hospitals all have a 24-hour accident and emergency department. Dublin Dental Hospital serves emergency dental needs and the Eye and Ear Royal Victoria Hospital has an out-patient surgery every day.
🖎 *Beaumont Hospital: Beaumont Rd, Dublin 9, 01-809 3000 • St James's Hospital: St James's St, Dublin 8, 01-410 3000 • St Vincent's University Hospital: Elm Park, Dublin 4, 01-277 4000 • Dublin Dental Hospital: Lincoln Place, Dublin 2, 01-612 7200 • Eye and Ear Hospital: Adelaide Rd, Dublin 2, 01-664 4600*

4 Medical Charges

EU visitors can claim free medical treatment in the Republic of Ireland if they have a European Health Insurance Card (EHIC) from their own country, available at post offices. To avoid paying for any treatments or prescribed medicines in the event of serious illness, you will need to show your EHIC and some identification, such as a passport. Make sure that the doctor treating you knows you have an EHIC. Visitors from outside the EU are advised to take out their own accident and health insurance before travelling or be willing to pay for treatment received.

5 Pharmacies

An extensive range of medical supplies is available over the counter at pharmacies but many medicines can only be obtained with a prescription from a local doctor. If you have, or are likely to have, any special medical needs it is worth having a letter from your own doctor giving the generic name of any medication you might require. Late night pharmacies are becoming more common.
🖎 *Hickey's Late Night Pharmacy: 55 O'Connell St, Dublin 1, 01-873 0427, www.hickeyspharmacies.ie*

6 Dentists

For emergency dental treatment you can go to the Dublin Dental Hospital in Lincoln Place. They also have an after-hours answering service giving appropriate information. Conor Gallagher dentist is happy to deal with visitor emergencies. 🖎 *Conor Gallagher: Fenian St, Dublin 2, 01-678 8158*

7 Personal Safety

Street crime does exist in Dublin, as in any capital city, but precautions should be taken to avoid any trouble. Avoid back streets or poorly lit areas at night. Don't carry around obviously expensive equipment, which will draw attention. If you are unlucky enough to be mugged or attacked, inform the police.

8 Theft

To avoid theft, don't leave things unattended in restaurants or galleries. If you have a car, lock everything in the boot (trunk) where it cannot be seen. The Irish Tourist Assistance Service (ITAS) provides support and practical assistance to victims of crime and can liaise with embassies, organise money transfers and ticket replacements, and cancel credit cards.
🖎 *6–7 Hanover St East, Dublin 2, 1890 365700, www.itas.ie*

9 Lost Property

The main bus and rail stations have lost property offices. In order to make an insurance claim you must report stolen property to the police immediately.

10 Street Begging

There are quite a lot of homeless people begging in the streets in Dublin, but they are generally unaggressive and it is a personal choice whether you give handouts or not.

Streetsmart

Left **The Shelbourne** Right **The Clarence**

Luxury Hotels

The Merrion
One of Dublin's finest hotels may seem unimpressive from the outside, but inside it is the embodiment of Georgian elegance, with ornate plasterwork, antiques, Irish fabrics and marble bathrooms. The modern world hasn't been forgotten – there is also a swimming pool, gym and business facilities.
🄈 Upper Merrion St • Map G5 • 01-603 0600 • www. merrionhotel.com • €€€€€

The Clarence
This 19th-century building has been spectacularly renovated by the Irish rock band U2, blending wood panelling with cutting-edge modern design. Located in the buzzing Temple Bar area (see pp18–19) and overlooking the Liffey, it is one of the most trendy places to stay in the city.
🄈 6–8 Wellington Quay • Map D4 • 01-407 0800 • www.theclarence.ie • €€€€€

The Shelbourne
From the moment you enter the wrought-iron canopied entrance to this beautiful hotel, greeted by the liveried doorman, you will be overawed by the grace and charm that have brought loyal customers here since the 19th century. 🄈 27 St Stephen's Green • Map F6 • 01-663 4500 • www.marriott.com • €€€€€

The Westbury
For 5-star luxury you can't do better than this Grafton Street hotel – the accommodation of choice for politicians and celebrities. It even has its own shopping mall if you can't face the crowds outside. 🄈 Grafton St • Map E5 • 01-679 1122 • www.doylecollection.com • €€€€€

Dylan
This luxurious boutique hotel in one of Dublin's most affluent areas is tucked away just off Baggot St, within walking distance of all the city's main attractions. The hotel is superbly stylish and charming, with impeccable service.
🄈 Eastmoreland Place • DART Lansdowne Road • 01-660 3000 • www.dylan. ie • €€€€€

Four Seasons Hotel
In the prestigious residential district of Ballsbridge, just 10 minutes by car from the city centre, is this luxury chain hotel with all the facilities one might expect: fitness centre and swimming pool, business facilities and 259 well-equipped rooms. A good choice if you want luxury away from the hub of the city. 🄈 Simmonscourt Rd, Ballsbridge • DART Sandymount • 01-665 4000 • www.fourseasons.com • €€€€€

The K Club
This 5-star hotel has two championship golf courses; designed by Arnold Palmer, they are considered to be among the finest in Europe. Rooms are luxurious.
🄈 Straffan, Co Kildare • Map P5 • 01-601 7200 • www.kclub.ie • Dis. access • €€€€

Morrison
Given that it was renovated by fashion designer and Dublin resident John Rocha, it is unsurprising that behind the Georgian façade of the Morrison hides an interior of supreme style. White walls, Irish carpets and contemporary art are some of its attractions. 🄈 Ormond Quay • Map D3 • 01-887 2400 • www. morrisonhotel.ie • €€€€€

The Fitzwilliam
This award-winning hotel, designed by the Conran partnership, boasts luxurious rooms and the largest roof garden in the country. 🄈 St Stephen's Green • Map E5 • 01-478 7000 • www.fitzwilliamhotel.com • €€€€€

The Davenport
Housed in a beautiful Georgian building, the Davenport has traditional style and elegance while offering all modern facilities. 🄈 8–10 Merrion St Lower • Map G5 • 01-607 3500 • www.davenport hotel.ie • €€€

Note: Unless otherwise stated, all hotels accept credit cards, have en-suite bathrooms and air conditioning

Price Categories

For a standard, double room per night (with breakfast if included), taxes and extra charges.

€ under €50
€€ €50–100
€€€ €100–150
€€€€ €150–200
€€€€€ over €200

Left **Brooks Hotel** Right **Trinity Capital**

🔟 Three- and Four-Star Hotels

1 The Gresham
Conveniently located on bustling O'Connell Street *(see p61)*, Dublin's oldest hotel has stunning Waterford crystal chandeliers which add a touch of elegance. ✪ *Upper O'Connell St • Map E2 • 01-874 6881 • www.gresham-hotels-dublin.com • €€€€€*

2 Herbert Park
A beautiful modern hotel, with floor to ceiling windows looking out over parkland. Contemporary Irish art decorates communal areas, including the lounge and restaurant. ✪ *Ballsbridge • DART Sandymount • 01-667 2200 • www.herbertparkhotel.ie • €€€*

3 Croke Park Hotel
This sophisticated city hotel is right across the road from the legendary Croke Park stadium, heart of Irish sporting life. It's a real hub on match days. The hotel offers shopping and theatre packages, as well as one that includes a tour of the stadium and the museum. ✪ *Jones's Rd • Any bus to Drumcondra Rd • 01-871 4444 • www.doylecollection.com • €€€*

4 The Morgan
All pale walls and beechwood furniture, the Morgan encapsulates the contemporary style of the Temple Bar area with its minimalist design. It can be noisy on the streets, so try for top-floor rooms. ✪ *Fleet St, Temple Bar • Map E3 • 01-643 7000 • www. themorgan.com • €€€€*

5 Jurys Inn Christchurch
A popular and very comfortable three-star hotel in an excellent central location opposite Christchurch, with Dame Street, Temple Bar, Trinity College and Grafton Street all just a short stroll away. The rooms are spacious and smart. There is also a hotel restaurant. A great base for exploring the heart of Dublin. ✪ *Christchurch Place • Map D4 • 01-454 0000 • www. jurysinns.com • €€*

6 The Schoolhouse
Converted from a 19th-century schoolhouse which saw some action during the Easter Rising *(see p31)*, many original features have been retained at this unusual 4-star hotel. Former classrooms have been converted into a restaurant and bar – fortunately the modern Irish food is far better than school dinners! ✪ *Northumberland Rd, Ballsbridge • DART Lansdowne Road • 01-667 5014 • www.schoolhouse hotel.com • €€€*

7 Brooks Hotel
With its dark wood foyer and bar and royal blue carpets, Brooks exudes old-world style. Downstairs, Francesca's restaurant has a more modern decor, reflecting a menu of modern Irish food. Set in a quiet street, the lively pubs and bars of Grafton Street are just minutes away. ✪ *Drury St • Map E5 • www.brookshotel.ie • €€€€*

8 The Spencer
A perfect city centre location to explore Collins Barracks, the Zoo and Phoenix Park. Relax in the heated pool, or take an exercise class before enjoying a slap-up meal in the American style steakhouse. ✪ *Excise Walk, IFSC, Dublin 1 • Map H3 • 01-433 8800 • www.thespencerhotel. com • €€€€*

9 Maldron Hotel Smithfield
This smart hotel presents great value in an excellent location. The local pub, The Cobblestone, is a classic, and there's an arthouse cinema next door. ✪ *Smithfield • Map B2 • 01-485 0900 • www. maldronhotelsmithfield.com • €€*

10 Trinity City Hotel
This hotel overlooking the walls of Trinity College has paid attention to every detail, combining Art Deco influences with a modern twist. Most striking are its oversized lilac sofas in the foyer, and wonderful sculptures. Excellent Irish breakfast. ✪ *Pearse St • Map F4 • 01-648 1000 • www.trinitycityhotel.com • €€€*

Left **Harrington Hall** Right **Trinity Lodge**

Townhouse Hotels

Hotel St George
The period staircase in this converted Georgian house is one of its most striking features, as well as the glistening crystal chandeliers made from Waterford glass *(see p83)*. The hotel is conveniently situated for all the literary sights north of the Liffey such as the Dublin Writers' Museum *(see p62)*. ◈ *7 Parnell Sq • Map E1 • 01-874 5611 • Dis. access • www.hotel-st-george. ie • €€*

Pembroke Townhouse
Every detail here exudes classic style, yet all the en-suite rooms are fully equipped with modern facilities including cable TV. Traditional Irish breakfast. ◈ *90 Pembroke Rd • Bus No. 10 • 01-660 0277 • www. pembroke townhouse.ie • Dis. access • €€*

Ariel House
Stately elegance and charming service are on offer at this Victorian house in a quiet suburb close to the city centre. Bedrooms are tastefully appointed in the period style. The guesthouse is a short walk from the Aviva stadium. ◈ *50-54 Lansdowne Rd, Ballsbridge, Dublin 4 • 01-668 5512 • www.ariel-house. net • Dis. access • €€€*

Harrington Hall
A collection of Georgian houses were combined together in 1998 to provide 28 meticulous rooms. The Irish breakfast is an excellent start to a day of sightseeing, and there is a private car park behind the hotel, which is always a bonus in congested Dublin. ◈ *70 Harcourt St • Map E6 • 01-475 3497 • www. harringtonhall.com • Dis. access • €€€€*

Eliza Lodge
A luxury, 18-bedroom guesthouse superbly located right in the heart of Dublin, overlooking the Liffey. The Temple Bar district is right on the doorstep. ◈ *24 Wellington Quay • Map E3 • 01-671 8044 • www. elizalodge.com • €€€*

Trinity Lodge
The 15 rooms of this Georgian townhouse are all elegantly decorated and fully equipped, while the communal rooms benefit from antique furniture. ◈ *12 South Frederick St • Map F5 • 01-617 0900 • www.trinity lodge.com • €€€*

Roxford Lodge Hotel
This elegant Victorian townhouse retains many charming original features. All the rooms are en suite and is situated only a short stroll from the city centre. ◈ *46 Northumberland Rd, Ballsbridge • 01-668 8572 • Dis. access • www. roxfordlodge.ie • €€*

Grand Hotel
Many rooms have lovely sea views in this large hotel, located in the charming and lively town of Malahide, which lies on the DART route along the bay. There are a variety of restaurants and pubs within walking distance, and the hotel has a heated swimming pool, jacuzzi and gymnasium. ◈ *Malahide • Bus No. 42, DART to Malahide • 01-845 0000 • www.thegrand.ie • €€*

Baggot Court
A short walk from St Stephen's Green and the shopping hub of the city on Grafton Street, this converted Georgian townhouse makes an unusual but attractive place to stay, as well as an affordable one. The price includes a full Irish breakfast. ◈ *Lower Baggot St • Map G6 • 01-661 2819 • www.baggot court.com • €€*

Waterloo Lodge
This renovated Georgian house with 17 en-suite bedrooms (including several family rooms), stands in the heart of one of Dublin's most affluent suburbs. The city centre and the Aviva stadium lie within walking distance. The lodge offers free parking, Wi-Fi and a complimentary cooked breakfast. ◈ *23 Waterloo Rd, Ballsbridge • DART to Landsdowne Rd • 01-668 5380 • www.waterloolodge. com • €€*

Note: *Unless otherwise stated, all hotels accept credit cards, have en-suite bathrooms and air conditioning*

Streetsmart

Price Categories

For a standard,	€	under €50
double room per	€€	€50–100
night (with breakfast	€€€	€100–150
if included), taxes	€€€€	€150–200
and extra charges.	€€€€€	over €200

Above **Number 31**

TOP 10 Guesthouses

1 Number 31
This unique hotel is comprised of two coach houses (converted by Irish architect Sam Stephenson in 1958) connected by private gardens to a classic Georgian house. With just 21 guest rooms it's a lovely place to stay, not least because all of Dublin's sights are within walking distance. ✪ *31 Leeson Close • 01-676 5011 • www.number31.ie • €€€€*

2 Windsor Lodge
This striking Victorian home is a haven from the hustle and bustle of the city. A short stroll from Dun Laoghaire with its many shops, bars and restaurants. ✪ *3 Islington Ave, Sandycove, Co. Dublin • 01-284 6952 • Map N6 • www.windsorlodge.ie • €€*

3 Aberdeen Lodge
A friendly and plush boutique hotel on a tree-lined avenue in salubrious Ballsbridge, Aberdeen Lodge serves delicious breakfasts and offers a wonderfully refined setting for a relaxing Dublin stay. ✪ *53–55 Park Ave, Ballsbridge • 01-283 8155 • DART Sandymount, Bus Nos. 7, 8, 45 • www.aberdeen-lodge.com • €€€*

4 Albany House
This 18th-century house was once owned by the Earl of Clonmel, but is privately run as a comfortable hotel, cleverly blending period furnishings with modern amenities. ✪ *84 Harcourt St • Map E6 • 01-475 1092 • www.albanyhousedublin.com • €€*

5 Kilronan House
Located in a glorious, leafy part of the city, this lovely, old-fashioned guesthouse is a short walk from St Stephen's Green and the National Concert Hall. The staff is friendly and welcoming. ✪ *70 Adelaide Rd • Map N6 • 01-475 5266 • www.kilronanhouse.com • €€€*

6 Waterloo House
This 4-star guesthouse is family-run and offers 19 fully equipped bedrooms in its four-storey Georgian house. It also benefits from a private car park, which is useful as the city centre is 10 minutes' drive away. ✪ *8–10 Waterloo Rd, Ballsbridge • DART Lansdowne Road • 01-660 1888 • www.waterloohouse.ie • Dis. access • €€€*

7 King Sitric
Better known as a fabulous fish restaurant *(see p77)*, the King Sitric also offers accommodation, with eight beautiful guest rooms, all charmingly named after local lighthouses and overlooking the sea. Enjoy the bustle of the city by day, then return to this haven of seaside calm. ✪ *East Pier, Howth • DART Howth • 01-832 5235 • www.kingsitric.ie • Dis. access • €€€€*

8 The Fitzwilliam
In the heart of Georgian Dublin, close to St Stephen's Green, this spacious town house has lots of charm and all the necessary mod cons. Friendly and relaxed, there are 13 en-suite rooms. ✪ *41 Upper Fitzwilliam St • Map G6 • 01-662 5155 • www.fitzwilliamtownhouse.com • €€*

9 Donnybrook Hall
This 4-star guest house is situated in the leafy area of Donnybrook, just south of the city. It is a family-run concern and is close to many of Dublin's best pubs and restaurants. All of its rooms are en suite and there are several quiet garden rooms and a comfortable sitting room. Free Internet access is available. ✪ *6 Belmont Ave, Donnybrook • Bus Nos. 10, 11, 46A • 01-269 1633 • www.donnybrookhall.com • €€*

10 Dublin City Inn
Excellent value for money right in the heart of the city. Pale floors, bright red sofas and a welcoming fire make up the lounge area, and the bedrooms are stylishly decorated too. The small garden at the back of the hotel is a wonderful and relaxing bonus in good weather. ✪ *95–98 Talbot St • Map F2 • 01-874 9202 • www.dublincityinn.com • Dis. access (family rooms) • €€*

Left **Waterford Castle** Right **Hunters Hotel gardens**

TOP 10 Waterford and Limerick Hotels

1 Clarion Hotel Limerick

This 17-storey, landmark hotel in Limerick is right on the waterfront and has great views over the Shannon. Its four-star facilities include a leisure club with swimming pool, gym, sauna and steam room. ⬧ *Steamboat Quay, Limerick • Map P3 • 061 444 100 • www. clarionhotellimerick.com • Dis. access • €€€€€*

2 Mount Juliet Estate

This 1,500-acre estate boasts an 18-hole golf course designed by Jack Nicklaus which hosted the WGC American Express Championship in 2002. There is also a spa and facilities for archery, clay pigeon shooting and horse-riding. Inside, the rooms are stunning and the two restaurants are award-winners. ⬧ *Thomastown, Co Kilkenny • Map P5 • 056 777 3000 • www. mountjuliet.ie • Dis. access • €€€*

3 Hunter's Hotel

One of the oldest coaching inns in Ireland, the Hunter's Hotel offers gardens, golf, tennis, horse-riding and fishing. Beaches are nearby and the restaurant takes advantage of the fresh fish for its traditional Irish cooking. ⬧ *Rathnew, Co Wicklow • Map N5 • 0404 40106 • www.hunters.ie • Dis. access • €€€*

4 Rathsallagh House

Once named the Country House of the Year, Rathsallagh House has an 18-hole championship golf course and is set on 530 lush acres of rolling landscape with several lakes, streams and woodland. On the west side of the Wicklow Mountains. ⬧ *Dunlavin, Co Wicklow • Map N5 • 045 403112 • www. rathsallagh.com • Dis. access • €€€*

5 Waterford Castle

One of the unique hotel experiences in the world. The 15th-century castle is set on a 310-acre island overlooking the River Suir. Access is by car ferry only and the hotel offers the very highest standards of comfort, luxuriously furnished with antiques and open fireplaces. ⬧ *The Island, Waterford • Map Q5 • 051 878203 • www. waterfordcastle.com • €€€€*

6 Adare Manor Hotel

Situated in one of the prettiest villages in the country, this 19th-century manor house is now a 5-star luxury hotel. Once the seat of the Earls of Dunraven, it is now American-owned. Good service is guaranteed. ⬧ *Main St, Adare Village, Co Limerick • Map P3 • 061 605 200 • www. adaremanor.com • €€€€€*

7 Butler House

Perhaps the most elegant place to stay in Kilkenny. This Georgian townhouse overlooks the river and Kilkenny Castle. Rooms are spacious, and sweeping staircases lead down to the well-maintained gardens. ⬧ *15–16 Patrick St, Kilkenny • Map P4 • 056 776 5707 • www.butler.ie • €€*

8 Cashel Palace Hotel

A grand hotel in a Queen Anne-style house that backs onto the ancient Rock of Cashel. You can expect a luxurious stay in rooms overlooking lush gardens. ⬧ *Main St, Cashel, Co Tipperary • Map P4 • 062 62707 • www. cashel-palace.ie • €€*

9 Richmond House

This 18th-century Georgian country house offers an award-winning restaurant and stunning grounds. Log fires warm period feature rooms. ⬧ *Cappoquin, Co Waterford • Map Q4 • 058 54278 • www.richmondhouse. net • €€€*

10 Hanora's Cottage

The Comeragh Mountains near here offer walking trails. Work up an appetite to enjoy the Irish cuisine of the restaurant. There is also a hot tub. ⬧ *Nire Valley, Ballymacarbry, Co Waterford • Map Q4 • 052 6136134 • www. hanorascottage.com • €€€*

Note: *Unless otherwise stated, all hotels accept credit cards, have en-suite bathrooms and air conditioning*

Price Categories

For a standard, double room per night (with breakfast if included), taxes and extra charges.

€	under €50
€€	€50–€100
€€€	€100–€150
€€€€	€150–€200
€€€€€	over €200

Above **Ashford Castle restaurant**

🔟 Galway and Connemara Hotels

1 The Twelve Hotel
This stylish four-star boutique hotel near the beach is nestled in the sleepy village of Barna. The luxuriously appointed rooms are individually designed, and there is a pizza kitchen and bakery shop as well as spa onsite. ◈ *Barna Village, Galway • Map N2 • 091 597000 • Dis. access • www. thetwelvehotel.ie • €€€*

2 Ashford Castle
This glorious castle is now a 5-star hotel and resort. Facilities include a health club with steam room, sauna and whirlpool. Available on the resort are golf, horse riding, falconry, cruising and fishing on Lough Corrib. ◈ *Cong, Co. Mayo • Map M2 • 094 954 6003 • www.ashfordcastle. com • Dis. access • €€€€€*

3 Delphi Lodge
One of Ireland's most famous fishing lodges. The atmosphere is elegant, with a library, a billiards room and a large drawing room overlooking the lake. Five restored cottages provide further accommo-dation. The surroundings are home to abundant wildlife, including falcons, badgers and otters. Fly-fishing offered for salmon. ◈ *Leenane, Co. Galway • Map M2 • 095 42222 • www.delphilodge.ie • €€€€€*

4 Ballynahinch Castle
Once home to the pirate queen Grace O'Malley (see p106), this casually elegant four-star hotel enjoys a breathtaking location, ringed by the Twelve Bens Mountains. The restaurant serves fresh game and fish. ◈ *Ballynahinch, Recess, Connemara, Co. Galway • Map N2 • 095 31006 • www.ballynahinch-castle. com • €€€€*

5 Cashel House
An oasis of calm in the wilderness of the Atlantic coast, this hotel rests elegantly amid beautiful gardens. Rooms look onto the gardens or the sea. Antiques and period paintings abound, as do open turf fires. Private beach. Walks, cycling, horse-riding and fishing are available. ◈ *Cashel, Co. Galway • Map N2 • 095 31001 • www.cashel-house-hotel. com • €€€€*

6 Ardagh Hotel
Located in beautiful Ardbear bay, this three-star hotel has 17 rooms, each with a private bathroom. If long walks amid Connemara's coastal scenery don't draw you here, the award-winning restaurant should. Open from Easter to October. ◈ *Clifden, Co. Galway • Map N1 • 095 21384 • www.ardaghhotel. com • €€€*

7 Currarevagh House
This country mansion, dated 1842, is situated right beside Lough Corrib in private woodland. Absorb the splendid isolation by walking in the woods, or take a fishing boat out. The house has a tennis court. Golf and riding are locally available. Open April to November. ◈ *Oughterard, Connemara, Co. Galway • Map N2 • 091 552312 • www.currarevagh. com • €€€€*

8 Foyle's Hotel
A lovely Victorian-era hotel that offers good, old-fashioned comfort, ease and charm. It has been in the Foyle family for nearly a century. Closed in January. ◈ *Main St, Clifden, Connemara, Co. Galway • Map N1 • 095 21801 • www.foyleshotel.com • €€*

9 Jurys Inn Galway
The Jury's chain offers good value well-placed accommodation. This branch is located beside the historic Spanish Arch overlooking Galway Bay. ◈ *Quay St, Galway • Map N2 • 091 566444 • www.jurysinns. com • Dis. access • €€*

10 Ballinalacken Castle Country House
The ruins of Ballinalacken Castle are right beside this guesthouse. The restaurant serves food by renowned chef Michael Foley. ◈ *Coast Rd, Doolin, Co Clare • Map N2 • 086 361 3719 • www.ballinalacken castle.com • €€€*

Left **Sheen Falls Lodge** Right **The Park Hotel**

🔟 Cork and Kerry Hotels

1 The Park Hotel
This hotel is in a 19th-century limestone building. Enjoy the restaurant's mix of classic and progressive cooking, while looking out over the 12-acre garden and Kenmare Bay. The hotel has a spa and is adjacent to an 18-hole golf course; salmon fishing and horse riding are available nearby. ❀ *Kenmare, Co Kerry • Map Q2 • 064 664 1200 • www.parkkenmare. com • Dis. access • €€€€€*

2 Sheen Falls Lodge
This rambling lodge is situated on a dramatic 300-acre estate above Sheen Falls and Kenmare Bay. The award-winning restaurant, La Cascade, overlooks a waterfall. The lodge has a fitness centre, swimming pool, billiards room and wine cellar. ❀ *Kenmare, Co Kerry • Map Q2 • 064 664 1600 • www.sheenfallslodge.ie • Dis. access • €€€€€*

3 Ballymaloe House
This ivy-covered Georgian guesthouse on a 400-acre farm is the best in its category. Enjoy the simply prepared food from the award-winning restaurant. Or try your hand at the small golf course, tennis court or splash around in the outdoor pool. Fishing and riding can be arranged. ❀ *Shanagarry, Midleton, Co Cork • Map Q3 • 021 465 2531 • www.ballymaloe.ie • Dis. access • €€*

4 Coolclogher House
Set in 60 acres of parkland, Coolclogher House is within walking distance of Killarney National Park. The large guest rooms have lovely views. The Victorian conservatory is built around a huge specimen camellia over 170 years old. ❀ *Coolclogher, Killarney, Co Kerry • Map Q2 • 064 6635996 • www.coolclogherhouse.com • €€€€*

5 The Old Bank House
Facing the bustling harbour, these two Georgian townhouses have been voted one of the "Top 100 places to stay in Ireland" every year since 1990. ❀ *10–11 Pearse St, Kinsale, Co Cork • Map Q3 • 021 477 4075 • www.oldbankhousekinsale.com • Dis. access • €€*

6 Castlewood House
A luxury guesthouse in which many rooms boast a stunning view out onto the bay. Breakfast is hearty and rooms are spacious and stylish. There's a lounge with DVDs and board games and some of the rooms have jacuzzi tubs. Hosts Helen and Brian are warm and gracious and ensure guests have a comfortable stay. ❀ *The Wood, Dingle, Co Kerry • Map Q1 • 066 915 2788 • www.castlewooddingle.com • €€*

7 Darby O'Gill's
This friendly family-run hotel is in a quiet rural setting five minutes' drive from Killarney town. Families are particularly well catered for. Traditional Irish music is played nightly in the summer. ❀ *Lissivigeen, Killarney, Co Kerry • Map Q2 • 064 663 4168 • www.darbyogillshotel.com • €€*

8 Aherne's Townhouse
This family-run pub is also a hotel and restaurant. The sitting room has an open fire and lots of books. Some rooms have balconies. ❀ *163 N Main St, Youghal, Co Cork • Map Q4 • 024 92424 • www.ahernes.net • Dis. access • €€€*

9 Shelburne Lodge
Once the home of Lord Shelburne (1737–1805), former prime minister of Great Britain. Informal, with log fire and wood floors. ❀ *Killowen, Cork Rd, Kenmare, Co Kerry • Map Q2 • 064 6641013 • www.shelburnelodge.com • €€€–€€€€*

10 Muckross Park Hotel
Set in Killarney National Park, this plush Victorian hotel is home to Cloisters Spa, winner of the Best Destination Spa in Ireland. ❀ *Muckross Village, Killarney, Co Kerry • Map Q2 • 064 6623400 • www.muckrosspark.com • €€€*

 Note: *Unless otherwise stated, all hotels accept credit cards, have en-suite bathrooms and air conditioning*

Above **Library Bar at the Everglades Hotel**

ᵀᴼᴾ10 Northwest and Northern Hotels

1 Coopershill

Set on a 500-acre estate of farm and woodland, this Georgian mansion lets you forget the world outside. Elegance is a virtue here, with candle-lit dinners served with the family silver. Along with the open log fires there are modern comforts, and peacocks wander through the garden. ◈ *Riverstown, Co Sligo • Map L3 • 071 916 5108 • www.coopershill.com • Dis. access • €€€€*

2 Temple House

The Perceval family have owned the house since 1665; the current building was refurbished in 1864. Rooms have a traditional atmosphere with log fires and canopied beds. The area has many archaeological sights and the hotel can advise on walks. ◈ *Ballymote, Co Sligo • Map L3 • 071 918 3329 • www.templehouse.ie • €€€*

3 Rathmullan Country House

Located on the quiet shores of Donegal, this country house also has award-winning gardens. Rooms are decorated in period style and family rooms and suites are available. There is an indoor swimming pool, steam room and tennis courts for added luxury. ◈ *Rathmullan, Co Donegal • Map K4 • 074 915 8188 • www.rathmullanhouse.com • €€€€*

4 Hilton Park

The Madden family have been resident in this grand house since 1734. The dining room is sumptuous beyond words, and the six bedrooms are superb with breathtaking views. ◈ *Clones, Co Monaghan • Map L4 • 047 56007 • www.hiltonpark.ie • €€€€*

5 Cromleach Lodge Country House

The lodge's unconventional design makes the most of the view overlooking Lough Arrow and the Bricklieve Mountains. A patio catches the sun and rooms all have great views, with a semi-traditional decor. There is a piano bar for the use of residents. ◈ *Castlebaldwin, Co Sligo • Map L3 • 071 916 5155 • www.cromleach.com • €€€*

6 Bushmills Inn

Once you check into this old coaching inn and mill house, you may find it difficult to leave. Not only will the open peat fires, pitched pine and gas lights make you want to stay, the Bushmills distillery – the oldest in Northern Ireland – in the village may make you forget how to get home. Golfing and fishing available nearby. ◈ *9 Dunluce Rd, Bushmills, Co Antrim • Map K5 • 028 2073 3000 • www.bushmillsinn.com • Dis. access • €€€*

7 The Crescent Townhouse

The chic end of Belfast's hotel market. There is a highly rated on-site brasserie and it is just a short walk to the Golden Mile. ◈ *13 Lower Crescent, Belfast • Map L6 • 028 9032 3349 • www.crescenttownhouse.com • €€€€*

8 Tyrella House

At the foot of the Mourne Mountains, Tyrella hides behind tall beech woods. Horse-riding and fishing can be arranged. ◈ *Downpatrick, Co Down • Map L6 • 028 4485 1422 • www.hiddenireland.com • €€€€*

9 Everglades

A luxurious hotel with an ideal location next to the River Foyle and beside the 17th-century walled City of Derry; it's also convenient for exploring County Donegal and the Sperrin Mountains. Satchmo's restaurant is well regarded. ◈ *Prehen Rd, Co Londonderry • Map K4 • 028 7132 1066 • www.hastingshotels.com • €€€€€*

10 Charlemont Arms

This modern inn attracts locals as well as visitors to its café/wine bar, one of the best in Armagh. Armagh's two cathedrals are nearby. ◈ *57–65 English St, Armagh • Map L5 • 028 3752 2028 • www.charlemontarmshotel.com • Dis. access • €€€*

Note: For a guide to price ranges in pounds sterling **see p117**

General Index

A

Abbey Tavern (Howth) 76
Abbey Theatre 40, 62
Aberdeen Lodge 131
The Academy 45
Adare Manor Hotel
  (Limerick) 132
Aherne's Seafood Restaurant
  and Bar (Youghal) 93
Aherne's Townhouse
  (Youghal) 134
air travel 120
Albany House 131
alcohol 123
All-Ireland Football Final 37
All-Ireland Hurling Final 37
Altamont, Earl of 105
ambulances 127
An Súgán (Clonakilty) 93
Annie's Restaurant
  (Ballydehob) 89
Antrim, Glens of 115
Aqua Restaurant (Howth) 77
Aran Islands Hotel (Aran
  Islands) 103
Áras an Uachtaráin 28
The Arches (Adare) 97
Ard Bia at Nimmos (Galway
  City) 103
Ardagh Hotel 133
Ardmore 83
Ariel House 130
The Ark 19, 36
Armagh 116
Ashford Castle (Cong) 133
Ashtown Castle 29
Athenry 102
Avoca, Vale of 81
Avoca Food Hall 47
Avoca Handweavers 57, 75
Avondale Forest Park 81
Avondale House 74

B

Bacon, Francis 61
Baggots Court 130
Ballinalacken Castle
  Country House (Doolin)
  133
Ballymaloe House
  (Shanagarry) 93, 134
Ballynahinch Castle
  (Ballynahinch) 133
Bank of Ireland 33, 56
banks 126
Bantry Bay 87
Bantry House (Bantry) 87, 89
Banville, John 35
Barnacle, Nora 34
Barrta Seafood Restaurant
  (Lahinch) 97
bars
  Greater Dublin 76
  South of the Liffey 58

Beara Peninsula 87
Beatty, Sir Alfred Chester 12,
  14, 16, 17
Beckett, Samuel 8, 35, 41
beer, Guinness Storehouse
  24–5
begging 127
Behan, Brendan 43
Beit, Lady 12
Beit, Sir Alfred 12, 70
Belfast 116
Bellucci, Giambattista 15
Belmore, Earl of 115
Belvedere, Earl of 99
Belvedere House 99
Bermingham, Meiler de 102
Bewley's Café Theatre 40
Bewley's Café and
  Restaurant 59
Bianconi (Waterford) 85
bicycles 37, 124
Birr 98–9
Birr Castle, Gardens and
  Telescope 98
Blackrock Market 47
Blair's Inn (Blarney) 93
Blarney Castle 92
Blessington 80
Bloomsday 41
Bog of Allen 74, 99
Bon Appetit (Malahide) 77
Book of Kells 8, 9
Bord Gais Energy
  Theatre 41
Bowen, Elizabeth 35
Boyle 112
Boyle family 23
Boyne, Battle of the 30
Boyne Valley 71
Brazen Head 43
breakfast 124
Brooks Hotel 129
Brown Thomas 57
Brueghel, Jan II 13
budget travel 124
Bunratty Castle 96
Burke, Edmund 8
Burke's Bar & Restaurant
  (Clonbur) 107
The Burren 95, 96
Burton, Decimus 28
buses 120, 121, 124
Bushmills Inn (Bushmills)
  117, 135
business hours 122
Butler House (Kilkenny) 132
Butler's Chocolate Café 47
The Button Factory 44

C

Café en Seine 43
Café Paradiso 93
Canova, Antonio 92
Caravaggio 13

cars 121, 122
  tours of Greater Dublin
  71
Cashel 95
Cashel House (Cashel) 103,
  107, 133
Cashel Palace 132
Cassels, Richard
  Gate Theatre 63
  Iveagh House 33
  Leinster House 32
  Powerscourt 69
  Rotunda Hospital 33, 66
  Russborough 70
  Trinity College 9
Castle Coole 115
Castlewood House 134
Castles
  Bunratty Castle 96
  Dublin 6, **14–17**, 32, 53, 55
Castletown House 69, 71
Castlewood House 134
cathedrals
  Christ Church Cathedral 7,
  20–1, 54, 55
  St Mary's Pro Cathedral
  66
  St Patrick's Cathedral 7,
  22–3, 54, 55
Cavendish, Lord 29
Cavistons (Sandycove) 77
Céide Fields 106
céilis 39
Celtic Note 57
Celtic traditions 39
Celtic Whiskey Shop 57
Celts 30
ceramics 125
Chambers, Sir William 9
Chapter One 63, 67
Charlemont, Earl of 74
Charlemont Arms (Armagh)
  135
Charles II, King of England
  29
Charles Fort 92
Chart House Restaurant
  (Dingle) 89
cheese 125
Cherry Tree Restaurant
  (Ballina Killaloe) 97
Chester Beatty Library **16–17**
Chesterfield, Lord 28
Chez Max 49, 59
Childers, Erskine 27
children 36
chocolate 125
Christ Church Cathedral 7,
  20–1, 54, 55
Christianity 30
Ciaran, St 98
City Hall 18, 32, 54
Clara Lara Fun Park 81
Clare 94–7
Clare Island 106

The Clarence 128
Clarion Hotel Limerick 132
Cleaver East 49
Clements, Nathaniel 28
Clifden 105
Cliffs of Moher 95
climate 122
Clonmacnoise 98
Coach Lane Restaurant
  (Sligo) 113
coach travel 120
Cobalt Café 63, 67
Cobbe, Archbishop Charles
  71
Cobh 91
Collins, Michael 14, 31, 43
Colours Boat Race 37
Comyn, Bishop John 22
Cong Abbey 101
Congreve, William 8
Connemara and Mayo 104–7
  hotels 133
  map 104
  restaurants 107
Connemara National Park 105
Conolly, William 69
consulates 122
Coolclogher House
  (Killarney) 134
Coole Park 101
Cooley, Thomas 18, 32, 54
Coopershill (Riverstown) 135
Copper and Spice (Limerick)
  97
Copper Face Jack's 44
Cork 90–3
  hotels 134
  map 90
  restaurants 93
Cork Jazz Festival 41
Cork, Richard Boyle, Earl of
  23
Cow's Lane 19
Crackpots (Kinsale) 93
craic 39
Cre na Cille (Tuam) 103
credit cards 126
Crescent Townhouse
  (Belfast) 135
crime 123, 127
Croagh Patrick 106
Crockets on the Quay
  (Ballina) 107
Croke Park Hotel 129
Cromleach Lodge Country
  House (Castlebaldwin)
  113, 135
Cromwell, Oliver 91, 106
crosses, Celtic 39
Crown Liquor Saloon
  (Belfast) 117
crystal 125
Cúchulainn 38, 39
Cullinans (Doolin) 97
Currarevagh House
  (Oughterard) 133

currency 126
Custom House 32, 61, 63
cycling 37, 124

D
Dalkey 75
Darby O'Gill's (Killarney) 134
d'Arcy, John 105, 106
DART 121
The Davenport 128
Davy Byrne's 58
Dawson, Joshua 56
37 Dawson St 58
de Valera, Eamon 31, 66
Deane, Sir Thomas 9
Deane's Restaurant (Belfast)
  117
Deerfield 29
Degas, Edgar 61
Deirdre 38–9
Delphi Lodge (Leenane) 133
dentists 127
Derry 116
Derrynane House 88
Designyard Gallery 57
Devil's Glen 81
Diarmuid 39
Dingle 87
Dingle Peninsula 86
Dinn Rig 39
discounts 122, 124
Djouce Woods 81
doctors 127
Donegal 112
Donnybrook Hall 131
Doyle, Roddy 35
drink-driving 123
driving 122, 123
Drumcliffe 109
Dubh Linn Gardens 15
Dublin Airport 120
Dublin Castle 6, **14–17**, 32,
  53, 55
Dublin City Inn 131
Dublin Fringe Festival 41
Dublin Horse Show 36
Dublin International Film
  Festival (DIFF) 41
Dublin Marathon 37
Dublin Theatre Festival 41
Dublin Writers' Museum 62,
  63
Dublin Zoo 28, 36
Dublinia 36, 56
Dunbrody Country House
  (Arthurstown) 135
Dunmore East 84
Dunne & Crescenzi 47
Durty Nelly's Oyster
  Restaurant (Bunratty) 97
Dylan Hotel 128

E
Earl of Thomond (Newmarket
  on Fergus) 97
Earls of Enniskillen 116

Easter Rising (1916) 31
L'Ecrivain 49
Edwards, Hilton 63
Eliza Lodge 130
Elizabeth I, Queen of
  England 9, 53, 91, 106
Ely Bar & Brasserie 67
embassies 122
emergency numbers 127
Emo Court 98
Ennis 96
Enniscoe House 133
Enright, Anne 35
Ensor, John 33
Epicurean Food Hall 47, 67
Everglades (Hotel) 135

F
fabrics, shopping 125
fairy trees 39
Fairyhouse Racing Festival
  37
Faithfull, Marianne 54
Fallon & Byrne 47, 59
ferries 120
Fiddlers Creek (Sligo) 113
Fionán, St 88
Fionn mac Cumhaill 39, 115
fire services 127
Fishers of Newtownmount-
  kennedy 75
Fishy Fishy Café (Kinsale) 93
Fitzgerald, "Silken Thomas"
  14
The Fitzwilliam 128, 131
Florence Court 116
Foley, John 8
food sellers 47
Fota Wildlife Park 92
Four Courts 32, 66
Four Seasons Hotel 128
Fowke, Francis 12
Foyle's Hotel 133
Foynes Flying Boat
  Museum 96
Francis Street 46
Friel, Brian 35

G
GAA Museum 66
Gaby's Seafood Restaurant
  (Killarney) 89
Gaelic football 37
The Gaeltachts (Gaelic-
  speaking areas) 84, 112
Gaiety Theatre 40
Gainsborough, Thomas 12, 13
Galilei, Alessandro 69
Gallarus Oratory 88
galleries see museums and
  galleries
Gallery of Photography 19
Galway 100–3
  hotels 133
  map 100
  restaurants 103

Galway City 101
Galway International Arts
    Festival 41
Gandon, James 54
    Bank of Ireland 33
    Custom House 32, 61
    Emo Court 98
    Four Courts 32, 66
    King's Inns 66
    Rotunda Hospital 33
Garden of Remembrance 66
gardens see parks and
    gardens
Gardiner, Luke 61
Gate Theatre 40, 63
General Post Office 62
George's Street Arcade 47
Giant's Causeway 115
Gibbons, Grinling 23
Gifford, Grace 26
Gladstone, William 31
Glasnevin Botanic Gardens
    and Cemetery 74
glassware 125
Glasthule & Sandycove 75
Glendalough 70
Glens of Antrim 115
Glenveagh National Park 109
Goldsmith, Oliver 8
Golf Club (Strandhill) 113
Gore-Booth family 109
Gort, Viscount 96
Gotham Café 36, 59
Government Buildings 56
Govindas 67
Goya y Lucientes, Francisco
    José 13
GPO 63
Grafton Street 46, 54–5
Grainne 39
Grand Hotel 130
The Grand Social 44
Grangecon Café
    (Blessington) 77
Grattan, Henry 31
The Gravity Bar 76
Great Famine 31
Great Music in Irish Houses
    Festival 41
Greater Dublin 68–77
    a drive around 71
    map 68
    pubs and bars 76
    restaurants 77
    shopping 75
Greenacres Bistro 85
Gregory, Lady Augusta 62, 101
The Gresham 63, 67, 129
Griffith, Arthur 31
guesthouses 131
L'Gueuleton 48–9
Guilbaud, Patrick 48
Guinness, Arthur 24, 25
Guinness, Sir Benjamin 33
Guinness Storehouse 7,
    24–5, 69

H
Ha'Penny Bridge 56
Half Door (Dingle) 89
Hall Walker, Colonel 70
Handel's Messiah 31
Hanora's Cottage
    (Ballymacarbry) 132
Harbourmaster 67
Harrington, Howley 18
Harrington Hall 130
Hartley's (Dun Laoghaire) 77
Haughey, Charles 31
health 127
Heaney, Seamus 35
Henry II, King of England 21,
    84
Henry, Mitchell 105
Henry Street 46, 63
Herbert Park 129
Hilton Park 135
historic buildings 32–3
history 30–1
Hodges Figgis 57
Hogarth, William 13
Hone, Nathaniel the Elder 12
Hone, Nathaniel the Younger
    12
Hook Peninsula 84
Horn Head 109
horse racing 37
hospitals 127
hostels 124
Hotel St George 130
hotels 128–35
    bars 123
    Cork and Kerry 134
    Galway and Connemara 133
    luxury hotels 128
    Northwest and Northern
        Ireland 135
    three- and four-star hotels
        129
    townhouse hotels 130
    Waterford and Limerick 132
House of Ireland 57
Howth 74
Hugh Lane Gallery 61, 63
Hungry Monk (Greystones) 77
Hungry Monk Café (Cong)
    107
Hunter's Hotel (Rathnew)
    132
hurling 37, 39
Hyde, Douglas 23

I
Ibn al-Bawwab 17
information sources 122
Inishbofin Islands 106
Inishowen Peninsula 109
International Bar 44, 58
Internet
    air travel bargains 120
    Internet cafés 122, 126
IRA 29
Irish Film Institute 19

Irish Museum of Modern Art
    (IMMA) 27, 76
Irish Tourist Board 122
Isaacs (Cork) 93
Iveagh Gardens 56
Iveagh House 33

J
Jam (Killarney) 89
James II, King of England 30
James Fox 57
James Griffin Pub 76
James Joyce Cultural Centre
    62, 63
James Joyce Tower 74
James Street South Bar and
    Grill (Belfast) 89
Jerpoint Abbey 83
Jervis Street Shopping
    Centre 46
jewellery 125
John, King of England 14,
    15, 84
John F Kennedy Park and
    Arboretum (Waterford) 84
John Paul II, Pope 29, 31
Johnnie Fox's (Glencullen)
    76
Johnson, Esther 12
Johnston, Francis 62
Johnston, Richard 33
Joyce, James 34
    Bloomsday 41
    James Joyce Cultural
        Centre 62
    Mulligans 42
    Sandycove Martello Tower
        74
    Stag's Head 42
Jurys Inn Christchurch 129
Jurys Inn Galway 133
JW Brasserie (Westport) 107

K
The K Club (Straffan) 128
Kavanagh, Patrick 35
Kealy's Seafood Bar
    (Greencastle) 113
Kehoe's 42
Kenmare 87
Kennedy, John F 42,
    84
Kerry
    hotels 134
    Kevin, St 70
Kevin & Howlin 57
Kilbeggan Distillery 98
Kildare, Earl of 23, 32
Kildare Village 75
Kilkenny Shop 57
Killaloe 96
Killarney 88
Killary Harbour 106
Killiney Hill Park 74
Killruddery House 74
Killybegs 112

Kilmacduagh Monastery 102
Kilmainham Gaol and Hospital 7, **26–7**, 69, 71
Kilronan House 131
Kilrush 96
King Sitric (Howth) 77, 131
King's Inns 66
Kinsale 91
Kinvara101
Koralek, Paul 9
Kylemore Abbey 105
Kylemore Abbey (Restaurant; Letterfrack) 107

L

La Bohème (Waterford) 85
La Dolce Vita (Wexford) 85
La Fougére (Westport) 107
Lady Helen Dining Room (Thomastown) 85
The Lakes, Blessington 80
Lakes of Killarney 87
Lambert Puppet Theatre 36
Lane, Sir Hugh 12, 61
language 39
Lansdowne, Marquis of 87
Lanyon, Sir Charles 8
Laytown Races 37
Leenane 106
legends and myths 38–9
Leinster House 32, 56
Lennox, Lady Louisa 69
Leopardstown Christmas Racing Festival 37
Letterkenny 112
Liberty Market 47
Lillie's Bordello 44
The Lime Tree 89
Limerick 94–7
    hotels 132
    restaurants 97
linen, shopping 125
Linnanes Lobster Bar (New Quay, Co Clare) 97
Lir, Children of 38
Lissadell 109
Listons 47
Lobster Pot (Carne) 85
Lobster Pot (Dublin) 48
Loch Erne, Lower 115
Londonderry 116
Londonderry, Marquises of 115
Londres, Archbishop Henry de 22
Long Hall 43
Longford, 2nd Earl of 99
Longueville House (Mallow) 93
Loop Head Drive 96
Lough Key 112
lost property 127
Lough Corrib 101
LUAS 121
Lynhams Laragh Inn (Laragh) 76

M

McCourt, Frank 35, 95
McDaids 58
McDonagh's Seafood House (Galway) 103
McGahern, John 35
McGuirks 75
Macha, Queen 116
Mack, Robert 33
MacLiammóir, Micheál 63
Maclise, Daniel 13
MacMurrough, Dermot 21
Maginni, Denis J 62
mail services 126
Malahide 75
Malahide Castle 74
Maldron Hotel 129
Malone, Molly 55
Malt House Granary (Clonakilty) 93
Mao (Dun Laoghaire) 77
Manet, Edouard 61
Mansion House 56
manuscripts, Chester Beatty Library 17
Marino Casino 74
The Market Bar 58
markets 47
Marrakech Eamon's (Lahinch) 97
Marsh, Archbishop Narcissus 23, 33
Marsh's Library 33
Mason, James 40
Mayo see Connemara and Mayo
Meath, Earl of 74
Meeting House Square 19
Mellon, Thomas 116
Merchant's Arch 18
The Merrion 128
Merrion Square 56
The Merry Ploughboy (Rathfarnham) 76
The Mill Restaurant (Dunfanaghy) 113
Millennium Bridge 18
Milltown, Countess 12
Mitchell's (Clifden) 107
Molly's Bar and Restaurant (Killaloe) 97
Monet, Claude 13
money 126
Montmartre (Sligo) 113
Moore, Thomas 81
Moore Street Market 47
The Morgan 129
Morris, Abraham 92
Morrison 128
Mosse, Dr Bartholomew 33, 61
Mount Juliet Estate (Thomastown) 132
Mount Stewart House 115
Mount Usher Gardens 74, 75

Mourne Seafood Bar (Newcastle) 117
Muckross Park Hotel (Killarney) 134
Mulligans 42
Murillo, Bartolomé Esteban 13
Murphy, Tom 35
museums and galleries
    Avondale House 74
    Dublin Writers' Museum 62, 63
    Foynes Flying Boat Museum 96
    GAA Museum 66
    Gallery of Photography 19
    Guinness Storehouse 7, **24–5**
    Hugh Lane Municipal Gallery of Modern Art 61, 63
    Irish Museum of Modern Art (IMMA) 27
    Kilmainham Gaol and Hospital **26–7**, 69, 71
    National Gallery of Ireland 6, **12–13**, 53
    National Museum of Ireland 6, **10–11**, 36, 53
    National Museum – Decorative Arts and History 66
    National Photographic Archive 19
    National Wax Museum 36
    Natural History Museum 56
    Skellig Experience 88
    Waterford Treasures at the Granary Museum 83
    Wax Museum 36
    Yeats Archive 12
musical instruments 39, 125
The Mustard Seed (Ballingarry) 97
My Museum 36
myths and legends 38–9

N

National Concert Hall 40
National Gallery of Ireland 6, **12–13**, 53, 55
National Museum of Ireland 6, **10–11**, 36, 53
National Museum – Decorative Arts and History 66
National Photographic Archive 19
National Stud 70, 71
National Wax Museum 36
Natural History Museum 56
Neary's 42
Nelson's Pillar 62
Newgrange 30, 70, 71
Newport House (Newport) 107
newspapers 126

nightspots 44–5
No Name Bar 58
North of the Liffey 60–7
  map 60
  restaurants 67
  walks 63
Northern Ireland 114–17, 122
  hotels 135
  map 114
  restaurants 117
Northwest Ireland 108–9
  hotels 135
Number 31, 131

O
O'Brien, Edna 35
O'Brien, Flann 42
O'Brien family 96
O'Casey, Sean 34, 40, 62, 101
Ocean Hotel (Dunmore) 85
O'Connell, Daniel 29, 31, 74, 88
O'Connell Street 61, 63
O'Connor, Roderic 12
O'Connor, Rory 21
The Odeon 58
O'Donoghue's 43
O'Dowd's Seafood Bar and Restaurant (Roundstone) 103
Oisin 38
Old Bank House (Kinsale) 134
Old Dublin 59
Old Jameson Distillery 63
Old Midleton Distillery 92
Oliver St John Gogarty 58
Olympia Theatre 40
O'Malley, Grace 106
101 Talbot 48, 67
O'Neills 58
One Pico 59
opening hours 122
Ormond, Duke of 29
Ormond, Earl of 23
The Osborne Brasserie Portmarnock Hotel & Golf Links 77
Osborne, Walter Frederick 12
O'Shea brothers 9
O'Toole, St Laurence 21
O'Toole, Peter 42
Oughterard 102
OX (Belfast) 117

P
Packies (Kenmare) 89
Paddy Burke's Oyster Inn (Clarinbridge) 103
The Palace Bar 58
Panem 67
Papal Cross 29
Park Hotel (Kenmare) 134
Parke, Captain Robert 112
Parke's Castle 112
Parkes, Richard 33
parking 121

parks and gardens
  Garden of Remembrance 66
  Glasnevin Botanic Gardens and Cemetery 74
  Iveagh Gardens 56
  John F Kennedy Park and Arboretum (Waterford) 84
  Mount Usher Gardens 74
  Phoenix Park 7, **28–9**, 69
Parnell, Charles Stewart 31, 74
Parnell Square 61, 63
Passage East 84
Patrick, St 22, 30, 106, 116
Peacock Theatre 40, 62
Pearse, Sir Edward Lovett 27, 33, 69
Pearse, Patrick 31
Pembroke Townhouse 130
People's Garden, Phoenix Park 28
Peploe's Wine Bistro 59
performing arts venues 40–1
petrol stations 121
pharmacies 127
Phoenix Monument 28
Phoenix Park 7, **28–9**, 69, 71
phonecards 126
Picasso, Pablo 13
Pichet 48
pickpockets 123
Pier 36 (Donaghadee) 117
Pins Gastro Bar (Galway) 103
Pitt Bros 59
Plunkett, Joseph 26
police 127
politicians 31
Pomodoro, Arnaldo 9
Poppies (Enniskerry) 77
The Port House 59
Portaferry Hotel (Portaferry) 117
Portarlington, Earl of 98
postal services 126
Powerscourt 69, 75
Powerscourt, Viscount 33, 55
Powerscourt Townhouse 33, 46, 55
Project Arts Centre 19, 41
pubs 42–3
  Greater Dublin 76
  The Purty Kitchen (Monkstown) 76
  South of the Liffey 58

Q
The Queens Bar and Restaurant (Dalkey) 76

R
radio 126
Raeburn, Sir Henry 13
rail travel 120, 121

Raleigh, Sir Walter 91
Rathmullan House (Rathmullan) 113, 135
Rathsallagh House (Dunlavin) 132
Reginald's Tower (Waterford) 84
rental cars 121
Renvyle House 107
restaurants 48–9
  budget travel 124
  Connemara and Mayo 107
  Cork 93
  Galway 103
  Greater Dublin 77
  North of the Liffey 67
  Northern Ireland 117
  Ring of Kerry and Dingle Peninsula 89
  South of the Liffey 59
  Tipperary, Limerick and Clare 97
  Waterford 85
  Yeats Country and the Northwest 113
Reynolds, Sir Joshua 13
Rí-Rá 45
Richard II, King of England 84
Richmond House (Cappoquin) 132
Ring of Kerry and Dingle Peninsula 86–9
  restaurants 89
Rinuccini (Kilkenny) 85
Ristorante Romano 67
road rules 121
Robinson, Mary 31
Robinson, Sir William 15, 26, 27, 33
Rocha, John 54
Rock of Dunamase 99
Romney, George 13
Rosleague Manor (Letterfrack) 107
Rosse, Earl of 98
Rotunda Hospital 33, 63, 66
Roundstone 106
Roundwood Inn (Roundwood) 76
Roxford Lodge Hotel 130
Royal Gunpowder Mills 92
Rubens, Peter Paul 13
rugby 37, 123
rush-hour traffic 123
Russborough 70, 71
Ryan's 42

S
Saba 59
safety 127
Science Gallery 36
Sea Safari 36
The Seafood Bar @ Kirwan's Lane 103

St Brigid's Crosses 39
St Mary's Abbey 66
St Mary's Pro Cathedral 66
St Michan's Church 66
St Patrick's Cathedral 7, **22–3**, 54, 55
St Patrick's Festivals 41
St Stephen's Green Shopping Centre 46
Sally Gap 80
Samuel Beckett Theatre 41
Schomberg, Duke Frederick 23
The Schoolhouse 129
security 123, 127
Semple, George 71
Shannon, River 96
Shaw, George Bernard 34
  Coole Park 101
  The Little Museum of Dublin 56
  National Gallery 12, 13
Sheen Falls Lodge (Kenmare) 89, 134
The Shelbourne 128
Shelburne Lodge (Kenmare) 134
Sheridans Cheesemongers 47
shopping 46–7, 125
  budget travel 124
  Greater Dublin 75
  South of the Liffey 57
The Silken Thomas (Kildare) 76
Sinn Fein 31
Sitric Silkenbeard 20
Six Counties 116
Six Nations Rugby 37
The Skelligs 88
Sky Road 106
Slieve Bloom Mountains 99
Sligo 109
Smirke, Sir William 29
Smithfield 66
Smuggler's Creek (Rossnowlagh) 113
Smyth, Edward 32
Sneem 88
South of the Liffey 52–9
  map 52
  pubs and bars 58
  restaurants 59
  shopping 57
  walks 55
The Spencer 129
Spiddal 102
sporting events 37
Stag's Head 42
Stapleton, Michael 33, 55
Stoker, Bram 8
Strongbow (Richard de Clare) 20, 21, 84
student discounts 124

The Sugar Club 45
Swift, Jonathan 8, 23, 34, 54
Synge, JM 40, 101

T
The Tannery (Waterford) 85
taxis 121, 123
telephones 126
television 126
Temple, Sir William 18, 19
Temple Bar 7, **18–19**, 53, 55
Temple Bar Food Market 47
Temple Bar TradFest 41
Temple House (Ballymote) 135
Terroirs 47
theft 127
Thoor Ballylee 102
Timoleague Abbey 92
Tintern Abbey 84
Tipperary 94–7
tipping 122
Tóibín, Colm 35
Tone, Theobald Wolfe 31
tourist offices 122
townhouse hotels 130
trains 120, 121
travel 120–1
  budget travel 124
travellers' cheques 126
Trevor, William 35
Trinity City Hotel 129
Trinity College 6, **8–9**, 53, 55
Trinity Lodge 130
Trocadero 49
Tuireann, Children of 38
Tullynally Castle 99
tweed, shopping 125
Twelve Bens Mountains 105
The Twelve Hotel (Galway) 133
Tyrella House (Downpatrick) 135

U
U2 54
Ulster-American Folk Park 116
Uno Restaurant (Enniskillen) 117
unsafe areas 123

V
Valdre, Vincenzo 15
Vale of Avoca 81
Valentia Island 88
Velázquez, Diego Rodríguez de 12, 13
Vermeer, Jan 12
Viking Splash Tour 36
Vikings 30

W
walking 121
  North of the Liffey 63
  South of the Liffey 55
water worship 39
Waterford 82–5
  hotels 132
  map 82
  restaurants 85
Waterford Castle (Ballinakill) 132
Waterford City Centre 83
Waterford Crystal 83
Waterford Museum of Treasures 83
Waterloo House 131
Waterloo Lodge 130
weather 122
Welles, Orson 40
Wellington Testimonial 29
The Westbury 128
Westbury Mall 47
Westport 105
Wexford Opera Festival 41
Whelan's 45
whiskey 125
White Gables (Moycullen Village) 103
Wicklow Gap 80
Wicklow Mountains 71, 80–1
Wicklow Town 80–1
Wicklow Way 80
Wilde, Oscar 34, 41
  Gate Theatre 40
  Merrion Square 56
  Trinity College 8
The Winding Stair 67
Windsor Lodge 131
Women's Mini Marathon 37
Woodhill House (Ardara) 113
Woodward, Benjamin 9
The Workman's Club 44
Wrights of Howth 75
writers 34–5
Wyatt, James 115

Y
Yamamori Noodles 59
Yeats, Jack B 12, 34, 109
Yeats, William Butler 34, 100
  Abbey Theatre 40
  Drumcliffe church 109
  Irish National Theatre 62
  Thoor Ballylee 102
  Yeats Archive 12
Yeats Country and the Northwest 108–9
  restaurants 113
Yeats Tavern (Drumcliffe) 113
Youghal 91

Z
Zoo 3, 28

Acknowledgements

Main Contributors

Polly Phillimore has worked as a freelance writer and editor for a number of years and with Dorling Kindersley for seven years. She moved to Ireland from the UK in 1995 and divides her time between Dublin and the West of Ireland.

Award-winning travel writer Andrew Sanger has contributed to a variety of newspapers, magazines and travel websites. From 1990–99 he was the editor of Rail Europe magazine, and is the author of more than 20 guidebooks, mainly on Ireland, France and Israel.

Produced by Sargasso Media Ltd, London

Project Editor Zoë Ross
Art Editors Philip Lord, Janis Utton
Picture Research Monica Allende
Proofreader Stewart J Wild
Indexer Hilary Bird
Editorial Assistance Nonie Luke

Additional Contributors
Robin Gauldie, Yvonne Gordon, Jason Mitchell, Christina Park
Main Photographer Magnus Rew
Additional Photography Joe Cornish, Tim Daly, Anthony Souter, Clive Streeter, Alan Williams
Illustrator Chris Orr & Associates

For Dorling Kindersley
Publishing Managers Jane Ewart, Fay Franklin
Publisher Douglas Amrine
Cartography Co-ordinator Casper Morris
DTP Jason Little
Production Melanie Dowland
Revisions Team Claire Baranowski, Marta Bescos Sanchez, Judith Bamber, Madhura Birdi, Tara Corristine, Kaberi Hazarika, Bharti Karakoti, Ciara Kenny, Shikha Kulkarni, Hayley Maher, Nicola Malone, Therese McKenna, Preeti Singh, Beverly Smart, Susana Smith, Ajay Verma, Nikhil Verma

Maps James Macdonald, Rob Clynes (Mapping Ideas Ltd)

Picture Credits

a-above; b-below/bottom; c-centre; f-far; l-left; r-right; t-top.

The publishers would like to thank the following individuals, companies, and picture libraries for permission to reproduce their photographs:

AKG, London: 34b; ALAMY IMAGES: Radharc Images 126tr

BALLYMALOE HOUSE: 93tl; BRIDGEMAN ART LIBRARY: Private Collection "*The Death of Cuchulain*" c.1940 by John Yunge-Bateman 38b, The Fine Art Society 38t; CHAPTER ONE RESTAURANT: 67tl, Joanne Murphy 48bl; THE CLARENCE: 49tl; CHESTER BEATTY LIBRARY, DUBLIN: 16tl, 16tr, 16b, 17t, 17b

COLLECTIONS: Michael Diggin 75tr, Image Ireland 134tr, Mark O'Sullivan 34tl, 41tr, George Wright 37tl; CORBIS: 1, 31cla, 50–51, 110–111, 118–119, Design Pics/George Munday 15cr; Courtesy of DART: / AFAomeara 121tr; Courtesy of DUBLIN BUS: 121tl

GLEESON'S: Julian Cottrell/ Alison Wickham 93tl; GLOWIMAGES: Destinations 21cra; GOTHAM CAFE: 59tl; GUINNESS STOREHOUSE: © 2002 Fennell Photography 24cb, 24b, 25t, 25cr, 25b, 76tr

HALO AT THE MORRISON HOTEL: 67tc; HASTINGS HOTELS: 135tl; HULTON ARCHIVE: 30tr

IMAGEFILE, Dublin: 28–9, 64–5, 72–3, 80tl, 80tr, 80b, 81b, 117t; IRELAND BLUE BOOK: 77t, 85t, 97t, 107t

LOCKE'S DISTILLERY MUSEUM: 98tr

MARY EVANS PICTURE LIBRARY: Jeffrey Morgan 35tl

THE MILL RESTAURANT: 113tl; Photos © NATIONAL GALLERY OF IRELAND: 6bl, 12–13, 13tr, Roy Hewson 12cl; © Michael Yeats " The Liffey Swim " by Jack B Yeats 12b," Christ in the House of Martha and Mary " by Rubens 13cr, " River Scene, Autumn " by Monet 13b

PA: 30tl, 31tr, 37tr; NATIONAL MUSEUM OF IRELAND, DUBLIN: Lensman 6tl, 10-11c; NIMMO'S:Rosie Lynch 103tl; RESTAURANT PATRICK GUILBAUD: Denis Mortell 48tl; RENVYLE HOUSE: 107tl; RETROGRAPH: 7cr, 24-25; REX FEATURES: 35tr, 35br; © 2001 SHEEN FALLS LODGE: 134tl; TOPHAM PICTUREPOINT: 31b; TROCADERO: 49tr; WHELAN'S: Aisling O'Neill 44bl; THE WINDING STAIR: 67tc.

All other images are © DK. For further information see www.dkimages.com

Acknowledgements

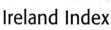

Ireland Index

Abbeyfeale	P2	Dingle	Q1	Louisburgh	M2
Abbeyleix	N4	Donegal	L4	Lucan	S2
Adare	P3	Doolin	N2	Lurgan	L5
Annamoe	T5	Downpatrick	L6	Malahide	U1
Antrim	K5	Drogheda	M5	Mallow	Q3
Ardara	K3	Dromahair	L3	Marino	T2
Ardee	M5	Drumcliffe	L3	Midleton	Q3
Ardglass	L6	Drumcondra	T2	Monaghan	L5
Ardmore	Q4	Dublin	T2	Monasterboice	M5
Arklow	P6	Dun Laoghaire	U2	Monasterevin	N5
Armagh	L5	Dundalk	M5	Mountshannon	N3
Ashford	U5	Dundrum	T2	Moy	L5
Athenry	N3	Dunfanaghy	K4	Moycullen	N2
Athlone	N4	Dungannon	L5	Mullingar	M4
Aughrim	T6	Dungarvan	Q4	Mulrany	M2
Ballina	L2	Dungloe	K3	Naas	N5
Ballinasloe	N3	Dunmore East	Q5	Navan	M5
Ballybofey	K4	Ennis	P3	Nenagh	P3
Ballycastle (Mayo)	L2	Enniscorthy	P5	New Ross	P5
Ballycastle (N.I.)	K5	Enniskerry	U3	Newbridge	N5
Ballyconneely	N1	Enniskillen	L4	Newcastle	U4
Ballyferriter	Q1	Ennistimon	N2	Newgrange	M5
Ballygawley	L5	Fermoy	Q3	Newmarket-on-Fergus	P3
Ballymena	K5	Foynes	P2	Newry	L5
Ballymoney	K5	Galway	N3	Omagh	L4
Ballymote	M3	Glencullen	T3	Oughterard	N2
Ballyshannon	L3	Glendalough	T5	Passage East	Q5
Ballyvaughan	N2	Glenealy	U5	Portadown	L5
Baltimore	R2	Glengarriff	Q2	Portaferry	L6
Bandon	Q3	Glin	P2	Portlaoise	N4
Bangor	L6	Gorey	P5	Portrush	K5
Banteer	Q3	Greystones	U4	Portstewart	K5
Belfast	L6	Hillsborough	L6	Portumna	N3
Belleek	L4	Holywood	L6	Randalstown	K5
Birr	N4	Howth	U2	Rathcoole	S2
Blessington	S3	Kanturk	Q3	Rathdrum	T5
Boyle	M3	Kells	M5	Rathkeale	P3
Bray	U3	Kenmare	Q2	Rathnew	U5
Bruckless	L3	Kilbeggan	N4	Rathvilly	N5
Buncrana	K4	Kilbride	S3	Redcross	U6
Bushmills	K5	Kilcar	L3	Robertstown	N5
Cahersiveen	Q1	Kilcolgan	N3	Roscommon	M3
Cahir	P4	Kilcullen	N5	Roscrea	N4
Carlingford	M5	Kildare	N5	Rosslare	Q5
Carlow	P5	Kilkenny	P4	Rostrevor	L6
Carrickfergus	K6	Killaloe	P3	Roundstone	N2
Carrickmacross	M5	Killarney	Q2	Roundwood	T4
Carrick-on-Shannon	M4	Killimer	P2	Sandycove	U2
Carrick-on-Suir	P4	Killorglin	Q2	Slane	M5
Cashel	P4	Killough	U3	Sligo	L3
Castlebar	M1	Killybegs	L3	Spiddal	N2
Castleisland	Q2	Kilmacanoge	U3	Sraghmore	T4
Castleknock	S2	Kilmacduagh	N3	Strabane	K4
Castlerea	M3	Kilrush	P2	Straffan	N5
Cavan	M4	Kinsale	Q3	Swords	T1
Clarecastle	P3	Kinvarra	N3	Tallaght	S2
Claremorris	M3	Knock	M3	Thomastown	P5
Clifden	M1	Laragh	T5	Thurles	P4
Clonakilty	R3	Larne	K6	Tipperary	P3
Clondalkin	S2	Leenane	M2	Tralee	Q2
Clonmacnoise	N4	Letterfrack	M2	Trim	M5
Clonmel	P4	Letterkenny	K4	Tuam	M3
Cobh	Q3	Limavady	K5	Tullamore	N4
Coleraine	K5	Limerick	P3	Tulsk	M3
Collooney	L3	Lisburn	L6	Waterford	Q5
Cong	M2	Lisdoonvarna	N2	Waterville	Q1
Cookstown	L5	Lismore	Q4	Westport	M2
Cork	Q3	Listowel	P2	Wexford	P5
Crossmolina	L2	Londonderry	K4	Wicklow	U5
Dalkey	U3	Longford	M4	Youghal	Q4